Healing Her Softly

ANN EVANS

Unless otherwise noted, all Scripture quotations are from the King James Version of the Bible.

AUTHOR'S NOTE: I do not claim to be an authority on any subject that has been preached or written by my colleagues of any faith or walk; it is just to share the experience of my own healing, which is the title of this book, *Healing Her Softly*.

Copyright © 2009 by E. Ann Evans
All rights reserved
09 10 11 12 13 — 987654321
Printed in the United States of America

ISBN 10: 1-56229-054-1
ISBN 13: 978-1-56229-054-2

Pneuma Life Publishing
www.pneumalife.com
1-800-727-3218

Tune in and watch Ann Evan's Broadcast
program on 24 Hour Internet TV Network
www.annevans.tv

Healing Her Softly
ANNE EVANS

Contents   *Pages*

PREFACE

Etrenda Ann Porter, that's what I always thought my name was. However, I experienced a shock when I went to get my driver's license and learned that my real name was Etrenda Ann Roberts.

As it turns out, Porter was the name of my mother''s first husband. So you can only imagine my shock when I learned that I did not have my father's name but my grandfather's name.

The most important thing for me is the name I received. When I married my first boyfriend and the father of my children, James I. Evans, I finally had a name! Someone finally wanted to give me his name. Now I know why Jesus gave us His name. He gave us His name for all the unwanted, unloved, and unnamed. Our Master gave us the right to His name, entitlements to everything He has, as His child, bride, and joint heir.

This is the beginning of healing to know someone loves you enough to give you his name and all that goes along with it. In turn we have to use the name! For every bill collector of hurt, heartache, lost rejection, and fear, He paid our debt and gave us a name that heaven, earth, and hell must honor.
Read on, and let Jesus begin *healing you softly…*

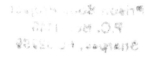

A Broken Little Girl…

Very much alone and afraid, the little girl lay crying in her bed as she heard her parents' screaming tirade through the paper-thin walls. What had she done wrong?

She used to come home eager to share happy stories from school, but lately she dreaded to open the back door. Would her mother be awake and playing the piano, or would she be passed out in a drunken stupor once again? And if she was once again dead to the world, whose house would the little girl go to? Some days she'd be so scared she wouldn't even stay in the house long enough to pack any clothes. She'd just run out the door and search for someplace safe to stay.

Some nights Dad would come home from work; other times he was away on business. Little did she know his business involved sleeping with women other than her mother.

The school nurse showed some when the little girl visited her daily with unbearable stomach pains, but day after a while it got to be a nuisance and concern. Finally, the nurse called her parents in for a meeting. As she watched her parents talk to the nurse through the glass windows in the school office, the little girl's stomach churned nervously. Breaking the code of silence meant trouble. Where had she gone wrong this time?

Some Sundays she went to a safe place where people told her about a man who performed miracles, but no one said these miracles were available to her. Instead, at her first Communion she was told by an angry priest, "I don't care if your parents are sick to death in bed; get on your bike and find a way to get to church every Sunday morning no matter what.

You're eight years old. It's your responsibility." There were lots of rules and prayers to memorize at this church, but the little girl was too afraid to share her fears or secrets with a man behind a curtain who yelled at her whenever she told him the truth.

No, she wasn't going to tell anyone she hid in terror in her closet when she heard her dad threaten to walk out and divorce her mother, who was passed out in a drunken haze. Four months later, she had been through four different schools and hadn't seen her mother because she was recovering in a hospital from a "nervous breakdown." Back then alcoholism wasn't a disease; it was a weakness.

At age nine, the divorce became final, and before her tenth birthday, she had a new stepmother just ten years her senior. Suddenly, she found herself in a new family with three small siblings. The little girl had become a big sister with many chores and responsibilities. There were kids to babysit and clothes to iron. There was no time for carefree play, no time to deal with her feelings.

During the summer, she went to visit her mother, who by this time had tried everything to stay sober. The girl was confused when she was asked to help sneak out garbage bags full of empty liquor bottles. She was angry when on her birthday she came out of a motel bathroom to find her mother's unconscious body, her head wedged between the bed and nightstand. As the ambulance carried her away, she didn't know if she was alive or dead. And if she had been true to her feelings at that very moment, she probably didn't really care. What about the time when she and her mom got a flat tire on the interstate, and her mom insisted she wait outside the car while she summoned help by talking to the annottuncers on the radio?

The not-so-little girl was terrified when her mother convinced her that her car and apartment where bugged by cameras and microphones, so, she'd better watch what she said and did at all times. This was crazy talk, or was it? Was her mother telling the truth about the abortion she'd had at age eighteen? Who and what was the young teen girl to believe?

Not wanting to get her mother into trouble, the young girl kept it all buried deep inside. It festered. But if she had shared her secrets, would it have kept the police from calling to say her mother had died drunk in a car accident? At age sixteen, she finally broke the code of silence when her step-grandfather molested her. She knew for sure the way he kissed and touched her was wrong. Did her confession bring healing and hope? Her dad threatened him with a gun, and if her stepmother hadn't hated her before this, she certainly did now.

The only thing that made the girl feel good inside was work. Working at her job. Working around the house. Working hard at school and achieving notoriety. She had become very successful at directing her negative energy toward something that society deemed as good—at least for a while.

But at age eighteen, even though she had promised herself to never let alcohol get the best of her as her mother had, she began a love affair with things of this world that soothed her raw emotions and forgotten feelings. She tried to help her best friend, whose father had been sneaking in and forcing her to have sex with him. She tried to forget her disgust in finding out her step-uncle had butchered a young coed and had been sent to jail for life.

When all of her personal effects were washed away by a devastating flood, she tried to be thankful that her family still had a home to live in. She tried to forgive the guy who slipped a Mickey in her drink at a party and raped her. But some days she was so tired of trying…

Chapter 01

THE CRY FOR HELP AND HEALING

HEALING HER
SOFTLY

I was so impressed this morning as I got up to pray. The scripture keeps coming to me out of the Gospel of John, the ninth chapter, verse 31. It says:Now we know that God heareth not sinners: but if any man be a worshipper of God, and doeth his will, him he heareth.

In other words, God doesn't hear the prayer of a sinner, but thank God He hears the cry of a sinner. Prayer is supplication, request, and talking to God. Sinners do not have that privilege. But God does hear the cry of a sinner: "I'm sorry." "I repent; please help me." The pleas of a two-year-old child learning to talk, babbling around a mother who doesn't pay that child much attention, are pretty much ignored. But when the child cries, immediately the mother goes to see what is wrong because that is an expression of desperation.

That's exactly where I was. In my own opinion, I was a good girl; I measured myself by the standards of people around me, but not by the standards of God. I went to Catholic school, I attended Mass on Sunday morning, and I went to the Baptist church in the evenings. But with all of that I still didn't know God. I didn't know that you had to be born again to enter the church; you couldn't just join it, but that's what I did. I had been called a whore most of my life by my stepfather. All of my mother's children were illegitimate, so he constantly reminded us all the time that we were going to be just like my mother. And so I began to fight that with everything in me.

But it seemed that all his predictions about me were right. By the age of fifteen I was already pregnant and getting married; that marriage with my first husband (who is now my husband) lasted about six years. I was beaten every weekend. I remember once having a broken nose and two black eyes for six months during my second pregnancy.

2

I went to the Catholic Church and pleaded with them for help, and the priest told me that was my lot. I went to the Baptist church and asked them what could I do. They told me what's sauce for the goose is sauce for the gander. That was the advice I got. I stayed in that marriage a little longer until finally something happened that broke the camel's back. And then I decided no more; I could not bear it anymore.

My husband was then in the service. We were traveling all around the country fighting everywhere we went. Everybody knew us because everybody had to come to our rescue and divide us and separate us. It took about six years before I would fight back, but finally I got to the point where I would defend myself. When my husband was transferred to Germany, I decided then that I would go back to school, get me a house, and educate myself so I could get out of this mess. And I did.

But it seemed that all his predictions about me were right. By the age of fifteen I was already pregnant and getting married; that marriage with my first husband (who is now my husband) lasted about six years. I was beaten every weekend. I remember once having a broken nose and two black eyes for six months during my second pregnancy.

I went to the Catholic Church and pleaded with them for help, and the priest told me that was my lot. I went to the Baptist church and asked them what could I do. They told me what's sauce for the goose is sauce for the gander. That was the advice I got. I stayed in that marriage a little longer until finally something happened that broke the camel's back. And then I decided no more; I could not bear it anymore.

My husband was then in the service. We were traveling all around the country fighting everywhere we went. Everybody knew us because everybody had to come to our rescue and divide us and separate us. It took about six years before I would fight back, but finally I got to the point where I would defend myself. When my husband was transferred to Germany, I decided then that I would go back to school, get me a house, and educate myself so I could get out of this mess. And I did.

I didn't know it was with the help of God. Before this I had attempted to commit suicide. In fact, all my life I'd thought about committing suicide. Suicide had been with me ever since I was a child, and I had made several attempts to kill myself even as a child. I didn't understand why, but there was always a compulsion in me to kill myself.

When I had gone back to my husband previously, even with the bad marriage, my family would have nothing to do with me; I didn't get any help from them. My husband had left me with no money in an apartment, and the baby had no milk., I thought to myself, "If I kill myself, my parents (meaning my aunt and my mother) will have to take care of my children." So I went outside and threw myself down the steps.

One of my neighbors, who were drunk at the time, came over and said, "Ann, I've been watching you. I know you've had a hard time, but God is going to help you." I didn't get that from any church or any other supposed Christian; it came through a drunk who, after she had said that, went back into her apartment. I said, "God, if You are God, and I don't know if You're God. From the way my life has gone I don't even know if You're God or if there is a God, but if You're God, bless me so I don't have to beg, steal, borrow, or become a prostitute to take care of my children."

4

With that I went back into the house, and the next day I got a job. It would be many years later before I realized that Jacob prayed a similar prayer. I didn't know it was scripture; I didn't even know that God had heard. I only knew from that point on I was able to support my children without financial aid from a husband or government officials.

That started a whole new training period for me. I went back to high school at night. I walked everywhere until I was able to buy a car. I got my first job in a telephone company, and I walked to work every day. I saved up my bus fare and brought my first car. During this transition, I was determined that I was not going to be a whore and no man would make a dish rag out of me.

My divorce was final by this time, and I married a second time. This man was the road manager for the light heavyweight boxing champion, so there was plenty of glamour and plenty of money for a while. Then he retired and the beatings started again. And when the beatings started, I left.

It seemed that was my lot—everywhere I went people wanted to beat me. But I determined that I was not going to be beat anymore. My mother's children also beat me. When my mother left, I had to leave the house as well because for some reason the children all attacked me, especially my brother. If my mother was gone eight hours, I had to stay out of the house eight hours if I didn't want to be beaten, even if it was cold or rainy—that was my lot. And so, I prepared to leave Chattanooga and my second marriage and go back home. I was working to have money so that I wouldn't have to stay with relatives when I got back to Florida. But while I was doing that, I got sick and had to be admitted to the hospital.

My first husband was visiting his niece in Chattanooga at the time. He heard that I was sick and was preparing to come back home, so he came and picked me up, brought me back to Tampa, and left again.

We went on, and by this time I was now into parties and the bar scene. I had a girlfriend who introduced me into this world, and I enjoyed it for a while. Let me back up a moment here. After I first got back from Chattanooga, I joined a church. My second marriage had gone bad and had lasted for about a month and a half, so I thought I needed God. So I joined a church, the church where the president of the school I had attended was a member. He was president of the usher board.

So I joined the church, trying to do this thing right again. One day the pastor said to me, ""You need to go to work so you'll stay in the church; go back and talk to head usher."" So I did. He said to me, "I'm so glad you're back in town; you need to be on the usher board, because right after the usher board meeting every Thursday night, we go to the bar." I looked at him and didn't respond, but I left that day. That was in 1973, and I never went back. I thought, "If this is all it is, then I don't need it. I can be good in myself, and I'm better than these people. At least I know what I am, and they don't."

For almost another ten years I was miserable, out of fellowship. My girlfriend invited me to church every Sunday. I never went with her because this was the same girlfriend who partied with me every weekend. And I love her, I love her dearly today. But I had no room for her God, because her God made no change in her.

In my opinion there had to be a change if there was God. And I saw no change in her life. It didn't mean I didn't love her; it just meant I wanted no part of her God because her God was not able to correct her and her lifestyle. Again I felt I was better than her; I was comparing myself with her because the things she'd do and then go to church were things I wouldn't do and then turn around and go. And that's dangerous, very dangerous. I find that what's wrong with so many of us today. We measure ourselves by peoples' standards and not by God's.

We went out again, and for some reason the walls of the club we were in that night were caving in on me. I turned around, looked at my girlfriend, and said, "I can't stand this tonight; get me out of here." As we were going out, somebody stopped her and asked, "What's wrong?" She said to them, "I don't know, but my girlfriend is going crazy. She's hollering to get her out of here." We went outside, and whoever she was talking to was outside also. When I got outside, I felt like I could breathe. I knew that night, for whatever reason, was my last bar experience

Outside the bar I met a man, and we went to dinner. He started to call me, and we continued to see each other. He later became my third husband. He was Mr. Perfect; he's everything that I had ever wanted. He supported me financially and emotionally, and he was good to my children. He also knew how to talk to me. All my life I had heard four-letter words, and even to this day I hate them with a passion; they sound to me like a gutter boiling up. I stayed away from anybody who would talk that way. But my third husband never used those words while we were dating; he was always polite, and we ended up married.

By this time I had worked myself up in Hillsborough County, where I was working. I was the second-highest paid black woman in the county. I had social standards and was respectable; I went to dinner with the commissioners. I had a good husband, but I was still miserable. There was still something missing in my life.

My husband got a promotion, so we moved to Ft. Lauderdale. When we moved, he said, "You don't have to work anymore." I couldn't believe it. At that time, I'd been working two jobs most of my life to make ends meet, and now I didn't have to work. My husband brought me a beautiful home and told me I could go back to college. I did, and I was still miserable.

Now we were partying, very sophisticated, not bars—but house parties with very important people and still getting drunk. But it was done nicely, so it was OK. So here we were. I got bored staying home, so I started looking for a part-time job. One of the ladies told me to come to Broward school board, so I did. I was hired, and that put us in another category of very sophisticated parties. My mother came down to visit me and said, "You know, you really ought to go to church." I said, "You're right," so again I went back to church. And again, immediately they wanted to put me to work in the church and I still wasn't saved. I joined the church and I was a good worker, but I still didn't know Jesus.

One day I came home from school and looked around my house. I had a beautiful home, a little money in the bank, beautiful furnishings, cars, credit cards, and everything. I walked in the house that day, and nobody was home. The boys had not gotten home, Jimmy wasn't home from work, and I said, You know, Ann, you ought to be happy.

You have obtained all of thislittle black high school dropout, pregnant girl. Look where you are, and yet you are not happy." There was still a void in my soul, and I said, What is this void? There is still something missing inside of me, and I don't know what it is.

And the devil said, "You need a Continental."

I said to myself, "That's right; that is exactly what I need. That will make me happy." I was still all centered on things. So when my husband came home, I told him what I wanted.So we started to look for this car. My girlfriend came down one Saturday, and she told me, "You know what, Ann? I think we need to have a Bible study." I agreed with her, so she continued, "I know this man (this is in 1979) who will give us a Bible study in our homes."I said, That sounds good; that way the guys can be included.

Then she continued, And by the way, he said that Jesus is black.I said to her, Mary I don't know who that man is, but he is not of God. You better leave that alone. She said, But we can try it.

I said, That is not of God. is no respecter of persons, and He loves everybody. Leave that alone.My husband came home, and she approached him with the same thing. His response to and Bible study was almost identical to mine. For some reason fear overtook her, and she said, I'm going home, because I did not know this man was not of God. You two do the same things that I do and you knew. There is something strange about you two, and I'm leaving. And she did.

9

The next month Jimmy and I both decided that we were going to church, and we did. We went to church Sunday morning and took the boys. We went to dinner Sunday evening and partied Sunday night, no change. We felt we were putting our good time in, so that excused how we lived our lives the rest of the time.

We were getting a little bit too close for comfort; a lot of the things we used to do we were stopping now. We wanted the boys to be involved in all these. because the church was really pushing the boys on. Nova (James Jr.) ha always been a gifted child. Keith was a natural leader, he in all the kids and church. we needed to be there to support the boys. As I said, this was a little bit too close for comfort for the devil.

Jimmy's company was planning a Christmas party, with company executives coming down from Philadelphia. We were invited to attend the party, and we knew the executives were over Jimmy because he was in line again for another promotion up north. It's a party where company executives made decisions involving hiring, firing, and promotions. So we went to the party that night.

There were only two blacks in the company in this position. One man had just moved down from up north, and Jimmy was the other one. So we sat down and began to play the little role game.

I don't know what happened to my husband that night. He was drunk, and I don't know how he got so drunk so fast. Let me back up again a moment and tell you about the warnings of God earlier that evening.

I put on a brand-new dress that night, and every seam in the dress tore; every seam split. I had to change dresses and wear one of my old black gowns. This made Jimmy angry because he always wanted me to look like perfection. To wear an old gown and have somebody know that I wore an old gown just wasn't his cup of tea, but my dress split. So I put on this old gown, did something to make it a little different, and we went on. He was arguing all the way there: "I told you to check your clothes."

Now we had to be by 6:00 p.m., because at 6:30 p.m. the bridge was going to be let up for a Christmas yacht parade; no cars could cross after the parade was over. We got to the bridge at a quarter to 6:00 p.m., and was already up. So he said, Well, I guess we are going to have to go home and miss this party and opportunity, and…" He continued with his arguing.

I didn't want to take the blame for missing the party because my dress , so I said, We can go down to Pompano and get over. So we raced from Ft. Lauderdale to Pompano and crossed over. By the time we sat down thirty minutes later he was sloppy drunk. I had never seen him so intoxicated in my life. As I went past the men's restroom, I could hear him swearing. I thought, "That's not my husband; something is wrong. He's embarrassing us, and he's embarrassing the company. I'd better get him out of here."

I suggested we leave and go home, and he said OK. We got down the stairs, and the language that started to come out of his mouth was just more than I could bear. I just couldn't believe it. I couldn't figure out what was wrong with him.

We got in the car, and on the way home he decided he was going to kill both of us. He ran off the bridge and ran in front of cars. With this happening and with his language, by this time I am frightened to death, but I'm still trying to figure out what is wrong with this man. How did he get so drunk, and where is this language coming from? This is not my husband. So when we got almost home I said, Please don't call me names; I can't take it!

He said, "Not only am I going to call you a name when I get you home," but he also told me what he was going to do to me. So when we pulled into the garage, I jumped out of the car and ran into the house to hide. I could hear him raging through the house, storming like a demoniac, just like a mad man. (That's what I thought that night even though I did not know the demoniac.)

This man was mad, he was kicking over things, slamming doors, yelling, and turning all the lights on. The boys sleeping, and I thought, "What in the world is wrong with this man?" We had a six foot bar in the back of our house, and I was behind there, stooped down and hiding.

Finally I got up and just sat there in the dark, because the boys were going to be up noise he was making and were going to be looking for me. I thought, "Whatever happens, I'm just going to have to take this and get it over with." At least with that somebody could get some sleep that night. So he found me and said, That was going to be the best Christmas we have ever had, "and materially it was. It was only the 15th or 16th of December, and on our back porch was the Christmas tree with barely room to walk with the presents he had brought. Bikes, microwave, I mean the tree was just loaded; there was hardly room to walk on the porch.

He started to kick the presents and knock them around, and I said to him, "What is wrong with you?" He said some more derogatory things to me, and I said, "If you have to talk to me this way, then I'll leave."

He said, No; you gone, take the boys too. His voice was a different voice; one voice was raging, and the next voice was like a little child who was lost or didn't understand it. By this time I was really fighting. The next voice said, "Leave," and with that I guess he hit me I don't know. I only knew somehow I was the bar and on the floor. Even today I don't remember how I got there. But I remember looking up at him as he was pouncing and hitting me and thinking, "One more time, God, one more time. This is my lot."And I said to myself, OK, you're tough, girl; you can handle this. You have handled beatings before; just lay there and take it."

And then I thought, "This can't be the same man." (All this is going through my mind while he is beating me.) This man has been so nice, so gentle. He's the one who gets up with my children. He's the one who goes to baseball and PTA meetings. I have not bathed myself in a year, one year, because it was my husband's delight to bathe me." The night before he had talked to me all night long, telling me how much he loved me.

Knowing this same man was about to beat my brains out didn't make any sense to me. I said, Jimmy, you are hurting me; do you know that you are hurting me?" And with that I screamed, which proved to be another mistake because my sons came out of their rooms to see what was going on, only to find their loving stepfather on top of their mother beating her.

My arm had gotten caught in the sliding glass door by this time, and I was black and blue and bloody. So my oldest son immediately came to my rescue, and I felt this man lift up off of me. When I looked at him didn't recognize face any longer. I blinked to try and focus, because there was no way possible that a human being's features could turn that way instantly. His eyes were red as blood, and he was foaming at the mouth. His back had humped over, and his nails had grown out. He was stalking my son like an animal, and I thought, "Dear God in heaven, what is this?"

My youngest son began to scream, "Help us! Somebody, help us!" I knew he was going to attack my oldest son, and I started to scream at him, "Don't hit him! Please don't hit him!" As he got close to him, I saw him when he hit. My son went to the top of our eight-foot ceiling, and he came down behind the chair. I just knew that he was dead and his neck had broken because of the way he was falling. I got up to see about my son, and by this time I was screaming. I heard all these screams and did not realize who all was screaming.

By this time my youngest son was in a panic. He kept screaming, "Somebody please help us." So I got to my youngest son and put him behind my back and tried to make it to the phone. But Jimmy had such supernatural strength that he ripped out the phone, the sheet rock, and everything. So I yelled to my youngest son go to the bedroom and call the police. By this time Keith got up from behind the chair. He was bloody and crying, but he wasn't dead. He ran toward me, and I pulled him behind my back. But all the fury that was me was now directed at this child. I remember going to the fireplace and picking up the fire poker, saying, "I got to stop him; I can't let him kill my child."

A voice said to me, "If you hit him with that fire poker, you are going to hurt him. You don't want to hurt him, do you?"

I said, "No, I don't want to hurt him, but I got to stop him. I can't let him kill my child." And I put the fire poker down. Keith and I were running all over the living room trying to get away from him, and finally we ended up in the kitchen. He came into the kitchen right behind us, and I remember looking through the drawers for something, anything to stop him with. And I ended up pulling out one of the kitchen knives.

He again started for my child, and I don't know if I stabbed him with the knife or if he charged the knife, but he was stabbed. I remember looking at him, and it was as if I saw the real Jimmy; it was like, "What's wrong, Ann? What's wrong?" I pulled his coat open, and there was blood.

I started to scream, and he said, Don't worry, suga momma; everything is gone be alright. With that he stumbled out into the garage and then into the car. I was frightened, but I wasn't going to go out to the garage where he was. But the child that he had tried to kill went out behind him.

I wasn't going out there—I didn't know if Jimmy, the monster, or whatever was out there. I didn't hear Keith though, so I got concerned and went and peeked the garage door to find out what is going on. I saw my son standing by the door and saying, "Oh get up Jimmy. Get up, Jimmy. Let me help you. Jimmy, please wake up; please wake up." When I saw my child had no fear of him, that gave me the courage to go the car also. We couldn't move him because he was a large man; he weighed over 200 pounds was over 6 feet tall. Since we couldn't move him, I slid under him and drove to the hospital—with him on top of me.

By the time I got to the hospital, my dress was wet with blood. Because it was a weekend during the holiday season, none of the doctors were on staff. There were only two RNs—and nobody to help us get Jimmy out of the car. We literally had to drag him out of the car into a wheelchair into the hospital. Then the nurses and I had to drag him a cart.

They had to send for a doctor, and by the time they got some-body to come out that time of morning it was too late. He had bled to death. They called for my minister, and he came to the hospital to see me. Never will I forget that there was nothing he could say, no prayer he could offer. He retired shortly after this incident. Because it was the holidays, most of the investi-gators were off from the police department. The captain of the investigation department came to the hospital. They had been to my home and sealed it off. They took custody of my children (my neighbor came down to the hospital and picked up Keith and Nova). Her husband also came later on. The police captain said, "We have to take you downtown," and all I can remember saying is, "I want my husband, I want my husband, I want my husband." He told my neighbor that he could drive me to the police department.

By this time I wasn't sure if this was a nightmare or if it was really real. . I remember walking through the jail and seeing all these people lying all over the floor. I wondered what I was do-ing here. I got to the man who was going to do the finger print-ing, and he looked at me and started to cry. I couldn't understand why he was crying. Then the captain said to him, "Don't worry; I'm not going to arrest this lady." And with that he proceeded with the finger printing process.

We went into his office, and he asked me some questions. I thought, "This is a nightmare, and I need to go to sleep so I can wake up and this will all be over." The captain must have realized what I was thinking, so he asked me if I was tired.

I said, "Yes, I want to go home."

He said, "I can't permit you to go home, but I will let you go to your neighbor's house." So he took me . I hurried to get into bed because I knew that when I went to sleep and awakened in the morning, all this will have been a horrible nightmare. My life was going to be normal again. I woke up that morning, and to my amazement that I was in my neighbor's house. I could look out my neighbor's windows the backyard of my house. I realized this was no nightmare. In one night my life had completely changed and almost been totally destroyed.

My sister was called, and she came down. We went to the house, and when I walked I collapsed. I knew then that it was no nightmare; this had actually happened. It was real. The police asked me to come back over the next day I. My sister took me to a hotel because she was afraid Jimmy's brothers were going to come from Tampa and try and kill me. We went to the police department, and when we drove up, they right behind us. They came over to the car and said, Ann, what can we do to help you?

I didn't want them to help me. I wanted them to be angry. I wanted them to kill me. I wanted them to be mad at me. My mother-in-law was on the phone with the police (she was too sick to travel); she said, I don't know what happened, but I know if my daughter-in-law this, there had to be a reason.

Please don't charge her with anything." My father-in-law came, and they were all pleading my case. And so the police did an investigation and released me.

Jimmy's funeral the most painful thing I have ever experienced in my life. Death, even of a saved person, is painful; death in this manner without God is almost unbearable. I remember in that funeral I was so angry with God, and this preacher was saying all these nice things about God. I was saying, "No, He is unfair. He is unjust."

My sister was taking tissues and stuffing them in my mouth, saying, "Ann, you don't want to blaspheme God." But I said, Look what He done to me all my life—heartache and pain I am angry with Him."

She said, "But you don't understand,you can question God. You do this." By they sedated me and brought me out. I woke up the next morning and went to the grave. I still could not believe this was true, so I started to dig up the grave with my hands and collapsed. I hit the coffin and knew again that it was real. I got in my car and thought, "This is over; I'm going to kill myself."My husband always kept guns in both of the cars under the seats.

I went for the gun, and the gun wasn't there. I then thought, "Ill go to my mother's house. She always has a house full of pills. I'll take them all." I went to my mother's house and let myself in. Every pill in her house was gone. I went to the silverware drawer to get a knife—but every knife was gone. I thought, "I can't even do this right; I can't even kill myself." And I just collapsed.

My sister had called the cemetery and had been calling around telling everybody to be on the lookout for my car. Since I was back in Tampa, a lot of people knew me. Someone called and said my car was at my mother's house. My sister rushed over and found me in a fetal position, curled up on the bed just wanting to die, just wanting to die. She said, "Ann, I'm going to take you and get you some help."

She took me to the hospital, they admitted me into the psychiatric ward, where later I had a complete nervous breakdown. And I wanted to have it. I wanted to be crazy because I did not want to deal with it. I had been pulling myself up by my own bootstraps and by my own strength all my life. one is too great; I have no more strength. I want to try any longer. Just let me die. Let me go crazy, don't let me have any strength.

And there were I was. Let me back up a little bit: I had been praying to die. That night my room turned pitch black, the blackest black I had ever seen in my life. I was not asleep, and as I was praying to God, this huge serpent came through the sky. The closer it got to me, the wider it opened up its mouth to engulf me. As it engulfed me, I could smell death and see little hands shooting out through all this darkness, as if they were pleading for help. I knew this serpent was coming for me and that was where I was going to be, and it frightened me. And I cried out, "O God, help me!"

HEALING HER SOFTLY by Ann Evans

Chapter 02

THE BROKEN LITTLE GIRL
INSIDE YOU

HEALING HER
SOFTLY

A child is about to be born of a woman. This blessed event is highly celebrated, frequently including a baby shower given for the expectant mother, with gifts for both her and the coming baby. Both the immediate family and the extended family await the birth. Such joy is anticipated by the mother and all those around her. What happiness the family experiences waiting for the bouncing baby to arrive.

In the fullness of time, the tiny baby is born; a new life is brought into the world. A healthy, beautiful baby girl enters life outside her mother's womb with cries and tiny hands in tight little fists. She is perfect and beautiful, having been created in God's own image.

A celebration of the cycle of life begins. The mother is so happy and so pleased with her tiny little darling. The father is thrilled; the family is proud and jubilant. Maybe brothers and sisters, if there are already children in the family of the newborn, join in the celebration. Happiness and joy abound.

The new baby girl is given a name so that she will have a unique identity. Her parents dress her up in cute little girl clothes and put ribbons, along with adornments, on her to show the world her never before seen special beauty. God has endowed this tiny girl with a beauty all of her own; no other of God's creations is exactly like her.

Everyone wants to hold this little baby; they want to kiss her and let her know how much she is loved by all those around her. This tiny baby is treasured, cared for, and loved. She is given dolls so she can learn to dress them up and make them just as beautiful and special as she is. She fixes their hair and puts adornments on them as she learns how to use these skills to make own appearance special an outward symbol of her own inner personality.

What a darling, precious little lady this baby is rapidly growing to become. She is her mother's heart and her father's pride and joy. She believes she can do anything and be anything she wants to become. She can accomplish any goal her heart desires. This girl knows she is beautiful inside and out. She knows her body is beautiful; her face shines with an inner glow from knowing how special she is—how much she is loved and valued by those around her. She knows that being female is a special joy that brings the favor of God. She even learns that she was created in God's image, and she treasures the fact that God, along with the angels, rejoiced when she came into the world.

The Little Girl Grows

The girl that was born in celebration and joy grows and begins to learn. She learns to read and write, and a whole new world opens up for her. She learns to count and read a clock. Slowly but surely, as she learns these new skills, society begins to enter into her world.

Soon this child learns things about the world outside her home. She learns that there are terrible things going on in the world. People hate and kill one another for no apparent reason. They hate each other because God created people with different shades of skin. They hate each other and try to keep others subservient to themselves—because of gender. Natural and man-made disasters leave people without homes; there is hunger, and many do not have enough food. This growing little girl learns that the world is a place of pain—pain as in child-bearing.

And she begins to realize that the joy of living is something wonderful in spite of the pain. Life began with pain; both mother and child must master the pain, but together they have the sweet victory of life.

Slowly but surely, the celebration of this child's life is over. She becomes just another person in a big, big world. Somehow her gender, so celebrated at first, becomes a burden. She becomes subject to the mores of society and religion.

Society tries to tell this girl what she can and cannot do, simply because of her gender. Society tries to tell her where she fits into the larger scheme of things. Suddenly the girl, once so celebrated because of her life and gender, finds that gender issues in the world actually hold her back, make her fit into a mold. What was so valued rapidly becomes devalued by the world.

Self-Confidence Erodes

This little girl, once so self-assured and confident that she could achievethat she could be whoever and whatever she wanted to becomebegins to realize the restrictions placed on her by society and even by religion. She once knew that she was special because of her gender. Now, slowly but surely, her gender begins to become more and more of a burden. She loses the self-confidence she had once enjoyed. She is no longer so certain that she is one of God's wonderful creations.

New words become part of her vocabulary—words like inequality, worthlessness, second class, incapable, object, and devalued. She learns that women can do the same work as men, but they do not receive the same benefits—all because they are not male.

She learns that society places a stamp that says "Devalued" on women simply because of their gender, regardless of how intelligent, how creative, and how capable they may be. This girl realizes that throughout history women have been bought and sold like merchandise in a store, and that, in many ways, the same practice is true today. She learns that women were often objects of great wealth—but only because of how men could use their bodies and because of the household services they could provide for men. She learned that in history, a woman was also valued for giving birth to a son, presenting a man with an heir. She learned that women who had beautiful bodies and faces were worth a great deal because of their beauty. She learned that intelligent women, even though attractive, were considered to be threatening by most men.

She also learned that, for many women, being a wife was a lot like being owned, not being a treasure. Men often took for granted that women loved and served them because God made women with the desire to help; God also created women to be willing to meet the physical needs of men just to hear "I love you; I need you." , sometimes with all to give, fulfilled one of greatest He needs me." This growing girl realizes that the feelings of women were often brushed off by the men they love; only feelings truly mattered.

The realization dawns on her that women were expected to keep a neat, clean home, have dinner on the table, give birth to children, and care for them (Gen. 3:16). While accomplishing all this, women were expected to work at low-paying jobs. Society expected the males to hold jobs and come home to enjoy the pleasures of their wife's labors, with very little else required of them. Yet women live the longest lives because of their great ability to forgive, even in sorrow and pain.

But Didn't God Create Woman?

This girl begins to realize that, while she had been taught in church that humans, both male and female, are created in God's own image, somehow women were being held captive by men, by society, and often even by religion.

Questions arise in the mind of this girl. God's Holy Word said that she was created in the image of God Himself, yet she is being told every day, through messages in word, in print, and in deed, that she is going to be forced to live her life under the shadow of second-class citizenship, males first. She is told that her life will be for the purpose of serving her world rather than serving God.

How can that be? Serving is not a problem; Jesus showed her when He washed His disciples' feet and when He said, "Well done, thy good and faithful servant." She doesn't mind serving, but she begins to wonder, "What has happened to all the celebration of my femaleness? Where has all the joy gone? Does God really expect me to be controlled by males, by employers who believe women do not deserve the same pay for the same work, and by churches that use scriptures taken out of context to make women feel subservient?"

Confusion sets in. She begins to she can trust God's Word what she is being told by people around her. She no longer knows what to think or how to act. She has been taught that God can be trusted. She wonders if this is true or if all the many conflicting facts pressed on her by society are, instead, the real truth. Something is clearly wrong, and she does not know what to believe anymore.

It is crystal-clear to this young woman that something is broken, but exactly what? Is it God's Word, or is it society? The girl wonders if God's Word is flawed, or if she is getting incorrect messages from the world around her. She begins to wonder, if the world is wrong, how she will learn to live with in a society that believes this misinformation. She realizes history indicates that these beliefs that women are unworthy and of little value except as servants to men are so deep-seated that her life will certainly be impacted by them. But, she wonders, what if God's Word is not really true, infallible, and inerrant? What if society is completely wrong but forces her to live under their value system? Where can she turn? What should she believe? How should she live her life? These questions and many others flood her mind.

The Breaking of Woman's Image

This happy little girl grows into a very unhappy and confused woman. She no longer has the feeling that she is special; that feeling is replaced by one of oppression. She no longer believes that she can do, that she can be, anything she sets her mind to; instead she hears society telling her what she can and can't do, what she can and can't become.

No longer does this little girl feel special and treasured. The reality of modern society sets in. This young woman realizes she has to fit into a mold made by people she doesn't agree with, and she doesn't get to make any changes to that mold. Over the years, she is manipulated, controlled, and used by men and other women. Her self-confidence is gone, and her self-esteem is lowered. She begins to believe that she is incapable and worthless. She begins to allow her body to be used by men in order to establish some degree of control over those men. She seeks escape—but there is no escape.

27

One day, she finds herself pregnant and alone. Now she has to live in the world of men, working at a degrading job for little pay and trying to support a child whose father has abandoned them. What remains of this woman's self-confidence and self-esteem slowly ebbs away. She feels hollow and falls into despair. This is the story of all too many women in the world today.

Does It Have to Be This Way?

Does this woman's story have to be the story of so many women's lives? No, it does not!

Are you tired of trying? Have you been there? Are you there? Do you know someone who is going there? Is your heart, body, and mind so tattered into broken pieces that you don't know which way leads to truth and healing? Have you used and abused yourself, others, money, drugs, and everything else in-between trying to fill that gaping hole in your heart? Do you feel numb—dead?

I am forgotten as dead man out of mind; I am like a broken vessel.
- Psalm 31:12

Is this you?

And when he had given thanks, he brake it, and said, Take, eat; this is my body, which is broken for you; this do in remembrance of Me.
- 1 Corinthians 11:24

Who is this? This is Jesus.

Sweet sister, our Lord Jesus wants to heal you. Re-read this scripture once again, and carefully notice whose body was broken for you. Who can relate to your brokenness no matter how bad, how painful, or how sickening or hidden it is? No matter where you have been broken—your heart, your vessel, or your spirit ,Jesus was broken to put you all back together again. Yes, our sweet Savior Jesus Christ.

Now, there are some of you out there who know exactly what I mean when I say Jesus, our Lord and Savior. Others have never been told about the possibility of having a personal relationship with God Almighty, Creator of heaven and . And when I say personal, I mean He wants to heal us, talk with us on a daily basis, teach us, cleanse us, and bless us. I'm not talking about a God who sits upon a mighty throne and judges and yells at us. I'm not talking about a God who can't relate to life's twists and turns. I'm talking about a God who lived on as a man, tempted in every way that we have been, a God who can relate to our insecurities, fears, anger, frustration, sadness, and disillusionment. I'm talking about Jesus.

But many of us are unable to get past our own pride that we can't reach God by our own devises, by our best effort or seemingly good deeds. Many can't accept the fact that we're all sinners. Believe it or not, from God's perspective, one person's sins are no better or worse than the next person's. Many people think, "My neighbor steals, lies, and cheats more than me, so I'm not that bad." But this is denial of our own sin. Despite how much God loves us, sinners cannot have a relationship with a holy God without atonement for their sins.

We must be willing to "'fess up" to our need for forgiveness. Once we say, "Yes, I am a sinner," what's next? We accept the free gift of atonement Jesus paid for us by dying on the cross for our sins. Our debt of sin has been paid once and for all if we accept by faith our need for Jesus. It's as simple as saying, "Yes! Jesus, I believe You died on the cross for my sins and that rose again. Please come into my life, forgive me of my sins, and lead me into life everlasting."

Once your heart has spoken these words, you are a new creation, and the Holy Spirit of the living God now resides in you—the same Spirit who lived in Jesus and brought Him up from the dead, the same Spirit who will lead you, guide you, comfort you, and heal your brokenness.

Now, some of you out there are saying, "I already know Jesus. I love Him, pray to Him, read my Bible, and have His Spirit, but I'm still broken." Maybe you're still carrying some heavy baggage in your spirit—a little unforgiveness , bitterness, hurt, denial, doubt, or anger in your heart. Some of you have forgotten what price Jesus paid for you. Others have forgotten that He can relate to your misery. Still others of us have missed our healing because we are waiting for a person to heal us instead of allowing our Jesus to heal us.

There are many definitions to the word broken. In Psalm 31:12, "broken" means your image has been broken. It means you have been so broken by situation and circumstances that you no longer know who and what you are. It's like the scripture in Isaiah 53 says; Jesus was marred and broken to the point where He could not be recognized as a man. By the time Jesus was on the cross, you could that He was a man because He was such a bloody mess.

30

It says that His beard was literally with such cruelty that it ripped the skin off His face and left it so bloody, so marred that a person could not stand to look at Him. That's what Isaiah means when he says Jesus was not comely, so nobody could look at Him. It didn't mean that He was ugly; a sinless God had to be beautiful. A sinless God had to be magnificent. A sinless God represents the glory of God, the purity and the righteousness of God.

You know how you look when you get cleaned up. You shine; what was dark to light. You know how you looked when you were full of sin; your lips were black, your eyes were black, your fingernails were black from all the reefers and cigarettes you smoked, and then all of a sudden God cleaned you up. Your fingernails got cleaned, your eyes got light, and the countenance of the glory of God came upon you.

You can't hide sin. I don't care how you slipped; you can't hide sin. You start slipping, and God is going to come on you. It's not going to be just your skin out there in the sun. The sun can't burn that kind of darkness, and I want you to know makeup and gold can't take it away! Nothing can take it away but the blood of Jesus!

"Broken" in Psalm 31:12 is a prime root word; it means "to lose oneself."

David's vessel was broken. David said, "I lost myself. I didn't know who I was any longer; I didn't know what I was supposed to be doing." Have you ever lost you? A whole bunch of us have lost ourselves, and we've been searching in all the wrong places trying to find ourselves.

31

We don't know what we are looking for because we are already broken. We go to other broken individuals in broken situations thinking that they can fix us, but they can't because they are broken and beaten up themselves.

"Broken," as in lost myself. My vessel was broken. I thought I could find myself in drugs or on sheets, with clothes or diamonds. I thought I could find myself by education. I thought I could find myself in my job. I thought I could find myself with another lover. But all of this didn't reflect who I am. Why? Because I am a child of God.

> Let's go back to the book of Genesis, to the beginning:
> In the beginning God created the heaven and the earth.
> - Genesis 1:1

The next verses go on to list all the things—including plants and animals—that God created. And after each day of creation, everything that God looked at after He had created it, He said it was good.

Then He said, "Listen, I'm pull a mirror out of My own self, because this creation that I'm now is higher than the angels, mightier than devils, and more majestic than anything this has ever seen. There's no copy of anything in , in heaven, or in hell that I to make My man, My woman in the image of My own self." Look at Genesis 1:26:

And God said; Let us make man in our image, after our likeness.Let's never forget this. We are created in God's own image. We aren't leftover trash. We aren't second-class citizens. We weren't created to sit up on a shelf and rot. The entire celebrated on the day we were reborn!

Now remember, God didn't take the woman from the dirt as He did man because He never wanted man to think he could walk on her. God took her from the heart to let the man know that this woman came out of God's heart.

> And the Lord God caused a deep sleep to fall upon Adam, and he slept: and he took one of his ribs, and closed up the flesh instead thereof; and the rib, which the Lord God had taken from man, made he a woman, and brought her unto the man. And Adam said, This is now bone of my bones, and flesh of my flesh: she shall be called Woman, because she was taken out of Man.
>
> -- Genesis 2:21-23

"You came out of my ribcage...you were lying next to my heart." The Bible says that out of the abundance of the heart the mouth speaks, and God said, "I couldn't produce this if it wasn't in My heart, so I'm taking her out of My heart, Adam, because I want you to understand and celebrate with e this creature called WOMAN!" (I will talk more about this and what a woman is in the next chapter.)

So what do we do as daughters of the Most High God? Do we celebrate our salvation? Do we study God's Word and renew our mind to who He says we are? Do we replace our stinkin thinking with His truth? If we don't start by admitting our brokenness and asking our sweet Jesus to heal us—to fill our mind and spirit with His Word—then we will never become all God has intended for us to become. Meditate daily on who He says we are:

1. I am God's child (John 1:12).
2. I am Christ's friend (John 15:15).
3. I am a saint (Eph. 1:1).
4. I cannot be separated from the love of God (2 Cor. 1:21).

5. I am a citizen of heaven (Phil. 3:20).
6. I am born of God and the evil one cannot touch me
(1 John 5:18).
7. I can find grace and mercy in time of need (Heb. 4:16).
8. I have been redeemed and all of my sins have been for
given (Col. 1:14).
9. I have not been given a spirit of fear, but of power, love,
and a sound mind (2 Tim. 1:7).

Have you surrendered your emotions, will and circumstances to God?Many times instead of surrendering, we try to hide behind fig trees and fig leaves in an attempt to cover our brokenness.

We have lost the image of who and what we were supposed to be. "Broken" means to break or to destroy. It means to fail. It means to be undone. It means to be void. I don't know why I'm here any more. That's why we are broken, because we don't understand our purpose. We don't understand our calling and the anointing.

You start to think, "I thought I was supposed to do this; well, I guess I'm not," because I ran into opposition. You think you can't do this any more because the enemy is trying to cause you to avoid what you are called to be. Don't let your circumstances cause you to avoid what you are called to be.

David was a man after God's own heart, and he called himself a broken vessel even after two anointings. Once God has put a little oil on every man and woman, all hell breaks loose. We cry out, "God, are You sure You have called me to do this? Are You for real, God?" We think, "It can't be God if it's this hard," because everything in our life has gone crazy.

You may be saying, "The church people have kicked my behind, my husband has given me gray hair, my children are acting like spoiled brats, and my family acts like they don't know me. I can't get anybody to pray with me. I can't get anybody to stand with me. God, I am broken. I used to have a little bit of pain, I used to pray for everybody else, but Lord, now I'm praying, 'Help me, Lord; keep me, Lord. Deliver me, heal me, be with me.'

"Everything around me and inside me is going through a stage of decay. I don't know whether to go right or to go left. I keep remembering that small voice that told me that I am a woman after God's own heart, but I don't feel like it, Lord. I don't look like it, and I don't act like it. Everybody is prospering but me, everybody is blessed but me, everybody is getting ahead but me. GOD, WHERE ARE YOU?"

Get to the height of your anointing. Maybe you'll be like Jesus on the cross— "'My God, my God, why have You forsaken me?' What did I do to You, God, that You leave me in my most critical hour? Where are You, God?

What did I do to deserve this? Did I sin? Did I backslide? Tell me, Lord; why have You forsaken me in my greatest hour of brokenness?"

Did you know that when you get to this point of brokenness and are really, truly honest with God about what you're thinking and feeling? When you are desperately crying out to Him— that's when He shows up in a big way? We have to be honest with Him. We have to let Him reveal our true heart's condition and not fake our way through it.

We have to come to the point of admitting we can't do this thing called life on our own. We need Jesus. Remember, God knows the number of hairs on our head. He keeps our tears in a jar. He knows what we need even before we ask for it.

When are we going to learn that brokenness is a good thing? It puts us in a place where we can admit our need to be put back together again. The Potter wants to put you back together again! You have to give Him time, and you have to be willing to get back on the spinning wheel.

The solutions have been provided to these issues right in God's Word. But we, imperfect human beings that we are, so often fail to heed the messages God has sent us in order to live a satisfying, happy life.

We as women have to study and learn how to live in modern society without letting the world direct how we think about ourselves. We can choose to let the world around us control our thoughts and actions, or we can follow God's Word and choose to live in love, happiness, peace, and worship. We must our value not by the voice of the serpent but by the voice of the Shepherd.

What choice have you made? Do you want to heal your broken image? Do you want to be truly happy, living a prosperous, satisfying life? Do you want to have eternal life in heaven once your life on Earth is over? These are important choices that will have an impact on every aspect of your life.
Learn to celebrate the life you have been given. We all have to overcome something—gender issues, race, education, class, money, or family relationships. God gives crowns for overcoming life problems.

Read the book of Esther. Queen Esther wore a crown, yet not a frown came when the call to save her people came from Mordecai. She was all attitude and purpose, no matter what others thought of her; she came to the kingdom for such a time as this, a God-directed time for serving mankind.

A God-directed life is true freedom: freedom from society's misshapen standards and morals, freedom from eternal suffering, both on Earth and in the hereafter, freedom from the hopelessness and despair experienced by the little girl who became a very unhappy woman. My prayer is that you will find that true freedom in God as you read this book.

HEALING HER SOFTLY by Ann Evans

Chapter 03

WHAT IS A WOMAN ANYWAY?

HEALINGHER
SOFTLY

In this chapter I must ask you to bear with me. It's long and on the technical side, but I feel this vital information is important for our understanding as we go forward in this book. Thank you.

What is a woman? What is her purpose here on Earth? To help us discover that, let's look at the definition of a woman, both from what W. E. Vine says about the word woman and its usage in the Bible and from Webster's.

In Vine's Expository Dictionary of Biblical Words, W. E. Vine gave a definition of woman from the Hebrew word 'ishshah:

'ishshah , "woman; wife; betrothed one; bride; each." This word has cognates in Akkadian, Ugaritic, Aramaic, Arabic, and Ethiopic. It appears about 781 times in biblical Hebrew and in all periods of the language.

This noun connotes one who is a female human being regardless of her age or virginity. Therefore, it appears in correlation to "man" (ish): "...she shall be called Woman, because she was taken out of Man" . This is its meaning in its first biblical usage: "And the rib, which the Lord God had taken from man ['adam], made he a woman, and brought her unto the man" . The stress here is on identification of womanhood rather than a family role. The stress on the family role of a "wife" appears in passages such as: "Go forth of the ark, thou, and thy wife, and thy sons, and thy sons' wives with thee."

In one special nuance the word connotes "wife" in the sense of a woman who is under a man's authority and protection; the emphasis is on the family relationship considered as a legal and social entity: "And Abram took Sarai his wife and Lot his brother's son, and all their substance that they had gathered..."

In <Lam. 2:20> 'ishshah is a synonym for "mother": "Shall the women eat their [offspring, the little ones who were born healthy]?" In <Gen. 29:21> (cf. <Deut. 22:24>) it appears to connote "bride" or "betrothed one": "And Jacob said unto Laban, Give me my wife, for my days are fulfilled, that I may go in unto her." <Eccl. 7:26> uses the word generically of "woman" conceived in general, or womanhood: "And I find more bitter than death the woman, whose heart is snares and nets..." (cf. <Gen. 31:35>).

This word is used only infrequently of animals: "Of every clean beast thou shalt take to thee by sevens, the male and his female: and of beasts that are not clean by two, the male and his female" <Gen. 7:2>.

This word can also be used figuratively describing foreign warriors and or heroes as "women," in other words as weak, unmanly, and cowardly: "In that day shall Egypt be like unto women: and it shall be afraid and fear because of the shaking of the hand of the Lord of hosts..." <Isa. 19:16>.
In a few passages 'ishshah means "each" or "every": "But every woman shall borrow of her neighbor, and of her that sojourneth in her house..." <Exod. 3:22>; cf. <Amos 4:3>. A special use of this nuance ouurs in passages such as <Jer. 9:20>, where in conjunction with re`ut ("neighbor") it means "one" (female): "Yet hear the word of the Lord, O ye women, and let your ear receive the word of his mouth, and teach your daughters wailing, and every one her neighbor lamentation."

Now let's look at how Webster's defines the word woman:

1 a : an adult female person b : a woman belonging to a particu-lar category (as by birth, residence, membership, or occupation) — usually used in combination *councilwoman*

2 : WOMANKIND

3 : distinctively feminine nature : WOMANLINESS

4 : a woman who is a servant or personal attendant

5 a chiefly dialect : WIFE b : MISTRESS c : GIRLFRIEND

Now that we know what the definition of a woman is, how did woman come to be in this big world we call Earth? How is it that she came to be created in God's own image? To learn that, we must go far back in time to the very beginning of humankind, to the Book of Beginnings called Genesis

In the Beginning…

God created the earth and all the things on the earth. "So God created man in his own image, in the image of God created he him; male and female created he them" (Gen. 1:27). It is quite clear that God created both man and woman in His own image. Every single thing that God creates is good and of great value. Both Adam and Eve were good in the sight of God, and He loved them both equally. They were created as equals to share the bounty of the earth.

What did God intend when He created these intelligent creatures, the humans? He created them in His own image to worship Him, to live in perfect happiness along with harmony, to enjoy the fruits of the entire garden (except one), and to multiply. He created them higher than the living beings called angels. Look at what Hebrews 1:6–7 says:

And again, when he bringeth in the firstbegotten into the world, he saith, And let all the angel of God worship him. And of the angels he saith, Who maketh his angels spirits, and his ministers a flame of fire.

How else could He join Himself to something not His own likeness or equal, not just to join but to marry?

How do we know this? Because God's infallible, inerrant Word, the Holy Bible, tells us these facts in Genesis 1:27–31:

So God created man in his own image, in the image of God created he him; male and female created he them. And God blessed them, and God said unto them, Be fruitful, and multiply, and replenish the earth, and subdue it: and have dominion over the fish of the sea, and over the fowl of the air, and over every living thing that moveth upon the earth.

And God said, Behold, I have given you every herb bearing seed, which is upon the face of all the earth, and every tree, in the which is the fruit of a tree yielding seed; to you it shall be for meat. And to every beast of the earth, and to every fowl of the air, and to every thing that creepeth upon the earth, wherein there is life, I have given every green herb for meat: and it was so. And God saw every thing that he had made, and, behold, it was very good. And the evening and the morning were the sixth day.

Notice that the sixth day, when mankind came on the scene, was called very good. Before that, the days were just good, but with man the days became very good. The sixth day is right before the day of rest, or the seventh day; six is also right before seven, the number of perfection.

When God created man, man was named "Adam." A is the first letter of the Hebraic language; "dam" is the blood, or to show blood in the face; we see this from Strong's Concordance. Therefore, Adam means the blood carrier of Elohim in the earth realm. Adam was the first to carry the blood of the Lamb as well as the first to have the DNA of God Almighty. Adam had the breath of God and was given dominion over all the areas of God's creation in the air, earth, and waters. His requirement was to obey, walk, rule, and commune with God. It is very important to note that after the Fall of man and the subsequent judgment and exclusion, Adam did not regress into something less; he was still in the image of God, with the breath of God inside of him.

But God didn't want Adam to be lonely; He wanted Adam to enjoy companionship. Therefore God caused Adam to fall asleep, and He created Eve in his own image—a perfect and wonderful creation, bone of his bone. Bones run throughout the body from the head to the toe, bringing support, strength, and structure. Whatever Adam would accomplish, Eve had the ability to help him. She also had flesh for his pleasure and to his liking—she was a help meet for him.

God's Word tells us in Genesis 2:21 that Eve, the first woman, was created from Adam's rib. This verse has been used by so many men to try to make women subservient to their wishes, not realizing the function of the rib. The rib protects the heart, as we see in Proverbs 31:11: "The heart of her husband doth safely trust in her [the one created from man's rib]." The rib is also the place of covenant—the reason we stand side by side in marriage.

PC Study Bible, *Vine's Expository Dictionary of Biblical Words, s.v.* "woman, OT:802," Copyright © 1994 Biblesoft and International Bible Translators, Inc. All Rights Reserved.

g sugar $1.49

① Tin of wraps $1.20

② Charm pops ¢28

① Dial soap $ 1.13+ ¢0.7 = 1.20

② Dial deodrant 1.08+1.08+¢0.14 = 2.30

④ Sodas 74×4 = $2.96

① bag peanut butter graham cookies $1.07

① Softee Bergamot $1.73+¢0.10 = 1.83

① moon pie ¢60

① Honey bun ¢49

God the Father tells Jesus the Son, "Sit on my right side." (See Psalm 110:1.) The rib is the place of joining, and it's the place where Jesus was pierced with the sword in his side on the cross. Can you see Adam being put to sleep and the Father raising his arm to remove a rib from his side? Can you hear the Father telling Adam, "Under your arms of protection, love, and respect I give you this woman"? Now look at the cross: under Jesus' arm we have the greater protection and love.

Adam and Eve were permitted to have dominion over and to enjoy all the things of the earth—except the fruit of one single tree, the tree of the knowledge of good and evil. God told Adam that the fruit of this one tree was forbidden, and if partaken of, it would result in death. Death was not a condition of human life as long as they obeyed God's explicit directions.

God was willing to allow Adam and Eve to enjoy His creations and worship Him as their main activity.But then an enemy entered the garden. Eve was the one who first fell for Satan's lies. Satan, posing as a serpent, started speaking to her as she stood next to the tree of the knowledge of good and evil. And she listened to his lies about her not being in the image of God.

He questioned her identity and caused her to desire something that she already was—the image of God. It is my belief that insecurity set in, along with comparison, and Eve felt that she had to embark on a search to become someone acceptable to her Father—forgetting the fact that all the time her Father was always before her.

PC Study Bible, *Vine's Expository Dictionary of Biblical Words, s.v.* "woman, OT:802," Copyright © 1994 Biblesoft and International Bible Translators, Inc. All Rights Reserved.

Both Adam and Eve ate the fruit of that one forbidden tree, the fruit of the tree of the knowledge of good and evil. Eve, and then Adam, chose to listen to the lies of Satan, and they chose to ignore God's instructions. Because of that, they had to pay the price for their choice to sin.

Sin entered the world at that time, and Adam and Eve were evicted from the garden. They had to work to survive and have food to eat. They were aware of their nakedness and had to make clothing to hide their nakedness. The pains of childbirth were introduced into the world, and the ever-continuing battle between good and evil began, the battle between humans and the minions of Satan that lead humans to do things that are against the will of God. That battle continues today, every single day, between Satan and every single woman and man living on Planet Earth.

Not only did sin enter the world, but death also entered— both physical and spiritual. The glory that once covered man and woman was removed, and they covered their selves with fig leaves that wither and die. And when God came walking in the garden searching for His creation, the Lifegiver, who had created all things good, had to cover His highest creation, who once wore His glory of light as brilliant as the stars (Dan. 12:3), with a hide, or skin, of an innocent animal.

Genesis 3:21 says, "Unto Adam also and to his wife did the LORD God make coats of skins, and clothed them." The Hebrew word for skins means "hide." God covered Adam and Eve with the hide of an animal.

PC Study Bible, *Vine's Expository Dictionary of Biblical Words*, s.v. "woman, OT:802," copyright ©
1994 Biblesoft and International Bible Translators, Inc.
All Rights Reserved.

Could this animal be the Lamb slain before the foundation of the world? After He covered them with love, He sent them out of the garden. Because of man, the God of life killed so others may live. Covering in God's kingdom has always been a place of love and protection with satisfaction, according to Psalm 91.

But then an enemy entered the garden. Eve was the one who first fell for Satan's lies. Satan, posing as a serpent, started speaking to her as she stood next to the tree of the knowledge of good and evil. And she listened to his lies about her not being in the image of God. He questioned her identity and caused her to desire something that she already was—the image of God. It is my belief that insecurity set in, along with comparison, and Eve felt that she had to embark on a search to become someone acceptable to her Father—forgetting the fact that all the time her Father was always before her. Both Adam and Eve ate the fruit of that one forbidden tree, the fruit of the tree of the knowledge of good and evil. Eve, and then Adam, chose to listen to the lies of Satan, and they chose to ignore God's instructions. Because of that, they had to pay the price for their choice to sin.

Sin entered the world at that time, and Adam and Eve were evicted from the garden. They had to work to survive and have food to eat. They were aware of their nakedness and had to make clothing to hide their nakedness. The pains of childbirth were introduced into the world, and the ever-continuing battle between good and evil began, the battle between humans and the minions of Satan that lead humans to do things that are against the will of God. That battle continues today, every single day, between Satan and every single woman and man living on Planet Earth.

PC Study Bible, *Vine's Expository Dictionary of Biblical Words, s.v.* "woman, OT:802," copyright ©
1994 Biblesoft and International Bible Translators, Inc.
All Rights Reserved.

Not only did sin enter the world, but death also entered—both physical and spiritual. The glory that once covered man and woman was removed, and they covered their selves with fig leaves that wither and die. And when God came walking in the garden searching for His creation, the Lifegiver, who had created all things good, had to cover His highest creation, who once wore His glory of light as brilliant as the stars (Dan. 12:3), with a hide, or skin, of an innocent animal.

Genesis 3:21 says, "Unto Adam also and to his wife did the LORD God make coats of skins, and clothed them." The Hebrew word for skins means "hide." God covered Adam and Eve with the hide of an animal.

Could this animal be the Lamb slain before the foundation of the world? After He covered them with love, He sent them out of the garden. Because of man, the God of life killed so others may live. Covering in God's kingdom has always been a place of love and protection with satisfaction, according to Psalm 91.

Women as a whole do not mind submitting to love or authority when they believe they are heard and respected as more than just flesh. God did not like the fact that Eve had sinned, but He did not hate His creation or feel that Eve was worthless because she had made a bad decision. He loved Eve. However, sin had a price. And God had a plan called redemption, and His woman would help carry it out.

PC Study Bible, *Vine's Expository Dictionary of Biblical Words, s.v.* "woman, OT:802," copyright ©
1994 Biblesoft and International Bible Translators, Inc.
All Rights Reserved.

The Needs of a Woman

What does a woman need? What are her needs?

Affirmation is a need for every human being, but especially for women. Affirmation tells a woman that she is accepted,
needed, wanted, appreciated and love. Affirmation is the first
thing God after He created man.

Three examples of affirmation are:
- Baptism of Jesus
- The church
- Marital relationships

Here are some affirmations a woman likes to hear:

- "Thank you; that was a job well done."
- "Thank you for going to work for me."
- "That was a very good meal. Thank you."

A woman needs admiration from her husband. She needs to
hear him tell her that she looks good, that she smells good, or in
other words, to flatter her. When this flattery is sincere, no problems will result; however, if a woman does not hear these words
of affirmation from her husband, they will be heard elsewhere.

A woman needs to be accepted for who she is as she is. She
needs to know that she is loved and appreciated. And she needs
hugs—and kisses.

- A kiss on the forehead says, "I accept your whole person." A kiss on the forehead promises protection and love, and it releases blessing.

- A kiss on the eyes says, "I never want you to cry in pain again. If you do, I'll be here to wipe away the tears."

- A kiss on the cheek says, "You make me happy. I'm glad you're my friend." A kiss on the cheek brings joy to the receiver.

- A kiss on the ear says, "I desire to be intimate with you and open your ears to hear my heart."

- A kiss on the lips says, "I approve of you. I need you. I'll be back."

Hugs are a language of love for women. When a woman is locked in an embrace and held tight, she feels secure. She feels safe and protected. Hugs and kisses are vital elements in meeting the needs of a woman. Life and love are expressed by communication, and hugs and kisses are vital in this expression of affection.

The Vagina Revelation

In the healing of women and myself, I found that I have become a drip of poison. I had died, dropped out of society, very much ashamed of who I was and what I was. It was not enough to be black, but I was a black female, which sometimes was thought to be at the lowest point of the totem pole in our society, a black female that was only good for pleasure and servitude, but never love, care, and provision.

So with that understanding, I discovered that I had a heart that wanted and longed for love, a heart tired of the violence against my nature by words by actions. I can honestly say that I have never been forcibly raped, but, of course, I have been violated. Violated to the point where pleasure was extracted from me but no pleasure was given to me. Violated to the point where my self-esteem, my sense of being female, my sexuality was torn and worn because of what I was not able to produce or feel because of my virginity.

I remember horrible things being said about my virginity. It took me years to get over that mental abuse; it made me close in. It made me became like that shell that covers an oyster. It made me be and become something I wasn't—very ugly on the inside and outside with something very precious on the inside.

All these hidden experiences are brought into the open without bitterness or anger just by naming them and turning them into positive actions and reactions for the necessary tool of living.

And the tool of living can only be enhanced by the precious gift of healing, which I think is what God wants us always to do. So sharing these things is as a bowel movement; it's releasing the toxins from within me so I can simply live without spreading toxins to others.

Little girls draw hearts on their notebooks. I dreamed of love and the picket fence and the prince that would take me away. We are mesmerized by this heart shape maybe because it is so much like our own bodies.

When we think about women, about their vagina, their clitoris and all these other things, we see a really power bundle that was created for their favor, something that we didn't know that was really blessed by God but hushed; we could not even mention it. It was called "down there," and "down there" was something that was dirty, something that was not to be mentioned or cared about. It was something that you didn't touch; you didn't want to know what it was. It was somewhere where someone else visited, someone else lived. It was not even a part of your body. It was just another part that was built for someone else.

Now with that understanding and with the clarification of what women are made for, we find in knowing that we can touch, we can talk; it frees up the memory of pain and it frees up the desire to love again. Being raped as little girls, teenagers, college students, and elderly women, we finally have a way of escape. Being beaten nearly to death by husbands…being taken sexually by stepfathers, brothers, and other males before we had conscience or will to say yes…we felt we had failed at life, when in reality it was society and life that had failed us.

When we fail to honor women…when we fail to protect the life that has been given…when we fail to feel safe, if we do not correct this, I believe it will be a end to us all. When you rape, beat, mutilate, and destroy the very essence of life and energy and the example of love and tenderness and nurturer, it means that now the protectors have become the hurters. What was meant to open up and let enter is now closed. What was meant to trust now is hiding. What was meant to nurture is now no longer able to nurture. And what was meant to be aliveis dead, broken, and frigid. It was meant to bring excitement, pleasure, and laughter.

We are so conscious of our need to be hurt, and now we are conscious of our need to be healed. It is time that we band together, and it is time that we simply just get healed. In order for the human race to continue, women must be safe, empowered, healed, and unveiled again. Like a vagina, it needs a great deal of attention and love in order to open up itself. The protectors must become healers and the wounded must become whole.

The wholeness in the first place is to find out where you are and what you are by not trying to become the protectors, but becoming who you are. Women go weeks, months, and sometimes years without even knowing who they are, without even looking at themselves. Isn't it something that men have an easy time looking at themselves. They look at themselves in the mirror. They look at themselves when they go to the bathroom. They hold themselves with pride that creates a sense of manhood, value, and self-worth. Every time there is release in their body functions, they are able to lay hands, hold what causes them to have a great sense of pride and sometimes even ego.

But women have to go in search to find ourselves. We actually have to take time to plan and examine ourselves, to look at ourselves, to know ourselves. Sometimes that can be very evasive and embarrassing for us, but we must understand it was created and we must take that time. It was an intention by God that we take that time to find ourselves, to look into ourselves, to know ourselves, to touch ourselves.

God intends for us to know that everything that was created by God was done for a reason. The hair covering the vagina is there to protect the friction of skin upon skin; it is there to portray the symbol of being a garden where growth and life can take place. It is there for the purpose of knowing, like the hairs on our head, they are counted and they are for glory. It is there so that the precious fruit within the garden can know that it is covered by grass and it can come up.

The vagina is not just a "down there" place, but it is a place that was created by God for reproduction, for pleasure, and, if you please, for beauty. With that understanding we understand that helping women to locate themselves, to love themselves, is to reclaim their center—the piece of her that is missing, the piece that is so given away that she doesn't know who she is. It is the opening for entrance, the closing to whole. It is life, and it's a body. In Psalm 139, we are told it is fearfully and wonderfully made.

Women are designed to be adored, and opening the vagina can bring one into extreme pleasure, and sometimes at the sacrifice of pain herself, and then to release life again at the sacrifice of herself. The body, the womb, is designed to hold a penis, carry a baby, take the penis in, and push the baby out.

Fearfully and wonderfully made is this creature, and her design was by the Almighty, opening and closing, closing and opening the garden, the center, a necessary door that releases that which even comes from heaven to earth like a John the Baptist, like a Jesus, like a you, like a me, like a King Solomon, like a David, like a Maya Angelou, like a Paula White, like so many various people, like the fastest runner on a field with a football team, like a Teddy Roosevelt. So many have come through the door.

The vagina is a practical place with biological terms, yet it is also a spiritual place that can house the gifts of salvation and the need of repentance. I have a heart that is in my chest; I also have one that is between my legs. Most of the things we have heard about he vagina are based on heresy—never really seen the thing, never wanted to see it. It never occurred to me that I needed to see it. But when something hurts, it's oddly that a woman has been torn from something she loves. Pain is not only in her chest, not only in the heart that beats within her chest, but it's the heart that beats between her legs.

Isn't that something the badger skin inside is all covered with red? No wonder the priest could enter now into that tent made out of badger skin through the three corridors walking in, but he had to back out much of the same way a penis has to back out. In backing out everything was enjoined; he sprinkled, and the sprinklings made the furniture one with him, one with what he had entered into and came out, causing the people to be one with his sprinkling.

For so long we have looked for a high priest who can come in us carrying sprinkles that enjoins us to everything around us, making us feel whole and accepted, beautiful and part of, equal not superior, not wanting to take over society.

That is not the heart of us either; I just want my place beside my man, and I think that is the heart of every woman. A place where I'm not looked down on or behind, but a place where I'm looked at as brains, beauty, and beneath. The brains can help carry out, the beauty will cause you to always look my way, and the beneath will carry you to places of ecstasy that you cannot and have never so imagined.

I come out of proving into acceptance your whole walk changes; in acceptance you just be. You don't have to prove anything; it is who and what I am. I am brains, beauty, and beneath. You will hear my brains, see my beauty, and lastly touch my beneath. Sometimes we as women think we cannot get involved in orgasms; we feel that it is wrong to be involved to manipulate, desire, or to tell, but when we learn to locate who and what we are, we can become involved.

The fantasy of someone having to always lead my life to choose my direction or give me an orgasm while I do nothing to give me pleasure while I do nothing is no longer the case. Now we can jump in, free to express our needs, our wants, and our desires— not in a demanding way, but in a teaching way by showing that we can no longer run from the needs that we obviously have to been created to have and to receive.

This is proven by our body part called the clitoris, which so many of us avoid finding. When we avoid finding it, we find ourselves frigid, dead, shut down, dry, bitter, and wondering, "Why, God? Why? Why am I here?" Life becomes a prison, full of hurts and pains that we have no explanation for. So many times we think that because of the state we are in, we have lost. We have lost our clitoris. We have lost our desire to be loved.

We have lost our need to be held or to be told sweet things, pretty things. We have to find out that when we thought we have lost our desire to be women, our desire to be desired, that's when we have lost ourselves. We find out biologically that we cannot lose what was built in us that God gave us. It is the doorbell to my heart; it is the entrance. We don't have to find it, but we do have to locate it.

Isn't that something the badger skin inside is all covered with red? No wonder the priest could enter now into that tent made out of badger skin through the three corridors walking in, but he had to back out much of the same way a penis has to back out. In backing out everything was enjoined; he sprinkled, and the sprinklings made the furniture one with him, one with what he had entered into and came out, causing the people to be one with his sprinkling.

For so long we have looked for a high priest who can come in us carrying sprinkles that enjoins us to everything around us, making us feel whole and accepted, beautiful and part of, equal not superior, not wanting to take over society. That is not the heart of us either; I just want my place beside my man, and I think that is the heart of every woman. A place where I'm not looked down on or behind, but a place where I'm looked at as brains, beauty, and beneath. The brains can help carry out, the beauty will cause you to always look my way, and the beneath will carry you to places of ecstasy that you cannot and have never so imagined.

I come out of proving into acceptance your whole walk changes; in acceptance you just be. You don't have to prove anything; it is who and what I am. I am brains, beauty, and beneath. You will hear my brains, see my beauty, and lastly touch my beneath.

Sometimes we as women think we cannot get involved in orgasms; we feel that it is wrong to be involved to manipulate, desire, or to tell, but when we learn to locate who and what we are, we can become involved. The fantasy of someone having to always lead my life to choose my direction or give me an orgasm while I do nothing to give me pleasure while I do nothing is no longer the case.

Now we can jump in, free to express our needs, our wants, and our desires—not in a demanding way, but in a teaching way by showing that we can no longer run from the needs that we obviously have to been created to have and to receive.

This is proven by our body part called the clitoris, which so many of us avoid finding. When we avoid finding it, we find ourselves frigid, dead, shut down, dry, bitter, and wondering, "Why, God? Why? Why am I here?"

Life becomes a prison, full of hurts and pains that we have no explanation for. So many times we think that because of the state we are in, we have lost. We have lost our clitoris. We have lost our desire to be loved. We have lost our need to be held or to be told sweet things, pretty things. We have to find out that when we thought we have lost our desire to be women, our desire to be desired, that's when we have lost ourselves. We find out biologically that we cannot lose what was built in us that God gave us. It is the doorbell to my heart; it is the entrance. We don't have to find it, but we do have to locate it.

We do have to lay back, mirror ourselves, and say, "This is who I am. This is what I am. And this is what I will be, and I will find a full satisfying life." Can you feel the warmth of life pulsating through you? Are you ready to live again?

Here's a statement for women by Natalie Angier:

The clitoris is clear in purpose; it is the only organ in the body designed purely for pleasure. The clitoris is a simple bundle of nerves, 8,000 to be exact. Eight is the number of new beginnings, eight is the number of where the woman is located on the breastplate by the tribe of Manasseh, causing me to forget all my pain, all my trauma, all my hurt that I have endured in my father's house. Eight thousand fibers, which is the highest concentration of nerve fibers found anywhere in the body, including the fingertips, lips and tongue. It is twice the number that is located in the penis.

As I started working on this book, I remembered being saved years ago, having come through so much tragedy in 1979. I had been beaten, almost left insane, almost looking at prison time, almost having my children not taken care of. There were just too many almosts, too many almost tragedies and too much hurt. I remember crying out and saying, "How can I live with this pain? What do I do to recap? There is no more strength." I could no longer pull myself up by my bootstraps, yet there was something inside of me that refused to let me die, refused to let me go, refused to allow me to give up. I had to develop a new love for myself.

Oddly enough, I hated what I had carried. I blamed my womanhood and my vagina for my pain. I thought that if I had no vagina, I would have no children and I would not have to see these faces look at me with confusion and wonder what happened. What happened to love, what happened to family, what happened to life. I remember not even wanting to go to the bathroom living with such a hate. A man was dead because of me, I was dead because of me, and my children were dying because of me. I did not want to touch the part that I blamed for all of it.

I remember being locked up in an asylum, wondering where God was. He came there and told me my answers could be found in my Bible. I needed to know what that was. Oddly enough the Bible started to talk about me. I had never heard about me. From what I had learned from the Scriptures, me the woman was the problem, the guilt, of all the problems of humans on the earth. There I found out that when God wanted to send a redeemer, a Jesus, a John, a David, a Boaz, a Esther, a Deborah he used an opening He had created and had in mind all the time.

In the study of this I began to appreciate my body. We are told by the Bible to love ourselves, and this includes the vagina. I realized that I could never love something that I thought was nasty and dirty. I realized that this part was made by God as much as my eyes and ears, my kidneys and my stomach, but it needed healing. I needed healing and was embarrassed by it. This may not be politically, socially, or even religiously correct, but I am just sharing how I got over, how I became healed on the pathway of life. In loving myself I rid myself of self-hatred, because no one can really receive love living in self-hatred or denial, repression, or hatred.

I remember praying in a hotel room one day before speaking at a church that evening, wondering what I was going to say to all those thousands of women. I remember so distinctively the Lord saying, "Ann, until you celebrate your womanhood, you can never really celebrate Me. In celebrating your womanhood, you say that I am God and I know who you are. You acknowledge that did create you and that you are fearfully and wonderfully made. I knew exactly what I was making when I formed you. You can enhance it or diminish it, but you can never say that I did not give it or create it.:

I thought I was incredibly ugly. I thought my vagina was incredibly ugly. That day I wished it wasn't there. It made me sick; how could anyone have gone down there? After all, it was just full of smell, channels, layers, and ugliness. But then that day, I had a new outlook about the way it felt, the way it smelled, the way it looked. Channels, layers, covenant—and it was not something that was ugly. It was sweet, pure and not to be destroyed by fear, by rape or even by disease. It was not to become a river of poison or puss and cause all that was in it to die, including me. It had been invaded, butchered, misused, not handled properly, treated attentively, but it was designed to heal and to be healed as all the body parts were and are, within the boundaries of grace, faith, and belief as well as medical science.

When God began to tell me His Word in a fearful and wonderful way, He said, "Come away, My beloved." The letters He wrote to Israel talking about His unfailing love, the psalms He wrote, how He used the prophets, how He used Hosea to woo after Gomer—I discovered that all of this was like foreplay to me, to convince me to try again. To believe that I was wanted, needed, and wonderfully made. Foreplay to convince me to get me to engage in a place of foreplay, of worship to get me to relax, settle down, and understand the nature of who I am.

It was kindness; the words were so kind from the page. I realized that I needed kindness. It had changed the way I thought about myself. My inner self and my outer self needed change. It was freedom from fables, heresy, error, and opinions. It was the silence, the confidence, the gentle kiss, the warmth that touched my inner being. I just wanted to be loved. I wanted someone to holding hands with, guiding me, walking beside me and pulling me into the place of trust. Holding hands means you are in agreement with the direction that life has for both of you.

The support system is in place, and as long as you hold my hand, I will never fail and we won't fail each other. Home for so many women has become a very scary place that they have fled, and now they are in places where they can't find safety, protection, and comfort. Our home should be a place of safety and protection; our covering should be our protection.

So many women don't have access to therapies, healings, or counseling, so they self-medicate themselves due to the lack of self-esteem with drugs, with prostitution, which many times cause death. Medication is only for those who say my pain it more than I can bear. For a woman who was designed to carry pain and deal with pain, the pain must be more surmountable than we can imagine. She can endure the pain of birth, the pain of rape, but how does she endure having to live with pain upon pain, care upon care? That's where I need the rivers to flow. I need the scrapping out, if you please, the emptying out. That's what the DNC is about, the scrape out and empty out. I must have a way to relieve, to express, to let go, to purposely let go. Remember she was designed to hold, the womb is designed to hold, so pain must force her many times to let go of what is hurting her.

If the baby did not grow and come to a place of such painful discomfort, she would hold it. She likes life being on the inside of her. The fight, the kicking, the push, the things in life begin to overwhelm her and invade everything, and now she is forced because of pain to push it out of her. The separation of pushing it out of her does not mean that she is not attached to it, but that she can no longer carry it on the inside of her.   This is the lesson that so many women need to know; sometimes the carrying becomes bigger than what we have room to carry, so we must push it out for the good of ourselves and of that thing so it can grow on the outside.

Yet we still have our attachments. Women we do not see who hurt and who need us—these are the women we must be healed for. So many times we have labeled our vaginas as a place of pain, nastiness, stench, invasions of blood, a site for mistakes and bad luck zone. Now we have to rename in order to reclaim. We have to take a look, we have to reshape, we have to empower ourselves by the knowledge of something greater than ourselves, more powerful than our society, more open-minded, because remember, women, if we isolate ourselves we are oppressed. Then we suffer confusion, confusion brings criticalness, and criticalness causes us to lose our focus on our society, on our survival.

Remember we were created especially for our God and for our man, not only to bring pleasure but also to be pleasure and to have pleasure so we can have a life full of desire. We do have brains, we do have beauty, and we do have a beneath. It's called a vagina, and to love it is to love yourself. Mentally we can no longer separate them.

Part One

The difference between the female and the male body physically is that female have breasts and a vagina. In my generation and in my family, the women very seldom talked about the vagina and the female genitals. They never called it by its proper scientific name. It was better known as the "pocket book," "box," "money box," and often with shame and embarrassment. Always with a slight pressure, this name is referred to the female as to what women really thought of the place that makes you "coo" while you crazy, "monkey" that made you something silly, "pocket book," or something that made you money—that you are not taking care of. Free of pleasure also was that the hope that it would happen, which brings us into our study on the female and the clitoris.

The clitoris is possessed by all females and only females. It is the only body part that comes with the female that its function is designed to bring pleasure. Their counterpart has dual functions, such as the release of pleasure and urine, but the female clitoris is only designed with no function other than for pleasure. This is so slight and overlooked; women don't understand their body function, and this often leads to where their problem ends. The physicians don't talk about it. Then, however, when we discover it, we learn how to massage, bring it to attention; therefore they say they know more about the women's body than the do women themselves.

Empowerment and self-knowledge about the body is a sense of freedom and intelligence. The attitudes about women's body have virtually been stemmed back to the 1960s—the baby boomer era (of which I am a member). Women in this scene have been sexual and have revolutionized the just-know available or the rape syndrome. In the 1950s women were known as "door mats," "rugs," and "pleasure machines" for men. Then in the 1960s the revolution of women said 'No!' to the not caring, 'No!' to the not feeling, 'No!' to not enjoying themselves as equal to their counterparts.

The 1960s were the evolutional stand. Women revolted sexually; they found out that their bodies also have pleasure and enjoyment. The early years of discovery are symbolic of the female finally discovering who she was, like she was, the nature and that nature of the purpose to examine her body and pay more attention to it both physically and emotionally.

Part Two

We discovered that women rebelled against female violence, that women raged against rape, physical abuse, harassment, and terrorism. Women were finding things. They were being healed by exposure. They would bring healing to areas that had been hidden. They opened up by naming the hurt, naming the pain, and turning their rage into positive actions. By doing so, it produced healing, freedom, and a sense of self-esteem. We call this the journey of truth, truth-telling. What was hidden for decades is now revealed because women have become tired of living in shame and in pain.

Oddly enough, in our study of this, I discovered that the clitoris is outside of the vagina. It has an outer course, an inner course, and then the sacred place, where miracles take place, where birth is given, and that place called the place of life. The woman's vagina is in the shape of an upside-down heart. It has point, a place of entrance; it has even the cherubim, which represent the ovaries on side. You come in one way and out the same way. You can bring life in and it will produce life. You can bring death in and it will produce death.

The shape of woman's uterus is almost equal to the shape of the human heart. Both have chambers being relatively the same and functions relatively the same. The producer of life. The giver of life. What comes in must go out; it must take in new life in order to keep functioning. In looking at the uterus and where it is, we discovered that those three areas of knowledge are vitally important. The female organs represent the place of the holy of holies. The hymen is the place where the veil is.

The hymen is called the martens head, the place that covers the opening, and this must be opened properly by praise and lubrication. If not, then it is torn and damaged, and usually forever shredded unless healed. So the painful remembrance of this can cause one foundation of improper sexual activities to be forever inhibited, but when the veil is opened properly like Jesus calls the veil to be opened, then the women is in a position now to enter into a the holy of holies and healing.

Unless the veil is open, even though it is entered with a jaggered cut and slithered with a cut of covenant, the cutting position is willingness, that position is care, that position is safety, that position is absolutely protection. So the veil is the first entrance, cutting the hymen. Usually in a virgin it bleeds, and it is not dead menstrual blood but blood of the covenant of entrance. And in the Hebrew time the blood was shed, the sheets would be shown the next day, which showed that this indeed was a virgin and proper covenant had been cut and established, that no one else had penetrated veil, that no one else had gone into an internal life exchange of blood and covenant had been established.

There is so much for us to learn, and in learning this it provides healing to own inner self. The vagina is the canal; it is lined by membranes on each side that extend a few inches and then connect to the entrance of the uterus. In a grown woman the vagina receives the sperm that the man places in during the intercourse. The vagina stretches widely when childbirth occurs, and we know that the newborn child comes through the vagina.

Enter in the internal female organs, which consist of the uterus, the cervix pointing down to the vagina, with two fallopian tubes and two ovaries. A channel, a canal, runs through the middle of the cervix up to the uterus. These things are in the middle of the uterus.

We understand that by this opening and what is functioning here that now you enter into three places. You first must enter in by understanding the nature of the clitoris, and that is why so many women find themselves in positions in what society calls as perverseness. What is understood or misunderstood is the nature of the clitoris with woman that it must be stimulated, massaged or nurtured. It is at that point, it is the outer court, that causes the egress to the inner court.

Part Three

Thanksgiving, of course, is the thing that causes the hymen to open up. Thanksgiving is even the thing that causes God to open up. Remember that individuals, including women, are made in the image of God. Man cannot respond properly without thanksgiving. Thanksgiving is the nature, the expression verbally of gratitude. What you are not grateful for can never be cared for properly.

Thanksgiving is what opens up the heart of God. Thanksgiving is what opens the heart of man. Thanksgiving then calls the hymen to be opened up and ready for the veil to be broken. Then the veil now has to be cut. We understand that in any surgical procedure, what is necessary is a shot, a clean instrument that causes precise incision without the spreading of disease.

We understand that the people who are in surgical rooms now have to be gloved, masked, and instruments have to be sterilized because they are entering through the very internal size of people. It is the same way that God created the need, the use, and the purpose of the penis, to be that surgical instrument that cuts inside, bringing life and healing. But to bring life and healing he has to place an actual stimulant on the woman that she would be desired to come inside of. And that desire, that need, is called the clitoris.

With that understanding take this picture now of a woman's body, her heart, not only in her chest but also her heart between her legs. We can therefore say she carries a heart between her legs; remember that the shape of the heart in the chest and the shape the heart between her legs are almost simultaneous in nature/similar in nature.

If you take your thumbs and put them together, and your two index fingers together, you make the shape of the uterus. When it spreads, it opens up and makes a heart. Even in school when we draw, you know the little pictures that kids draw, with the hearts, they catch themselves drawing the shape of the heart symbolizes the uterus upsidedown. So here is the uterus; it must be entered the same way as entering the temple—one way in, one way out; coming in bringing life, or coming in and bringing death. So now we understand the nature of the woman—when she gives her body, really giving her heart, one does not penetrate her body usually not penetrating her very heart. That is why her hurt goes so much deeper and takes usually so much longer to heal because she is actually penetrated. Her veil, hymen, has been penetrated, and the man has entered into her vagina, and now you are in the place of her cervix, the final place.

Cervical cancer is at an all-time high. Why? That is the place of the altar. That is the place where you leave your deposit, whether it is life or death. So now you have three places, just like in the temple: the hymen—cutting the veil, entering into the vagina, and then resting at the place of the cervix. With the entrance of the clitoris so many women find themselves not into pleasure simply because men don't know how to stimulate the clitoris, which is a pleasure point. He does not understand that without stimulation of the outer cord, he can never meet the fulfillment of the inner cord.

Part Four

The hymen stretches across the entrance to the vagina; it has membranes so that the menstrual fluid can flow during the menstruation period. Remember it is the veil that covers the vagina, the symbolic veil; it is the veil that protects it until it is time to be opened and penetrated. It opens, of course, to relax itself to praise, it becomes lubricated, and it becomes red—just like the veil in the temple. Remember when Jesus was crucified; the veil was red, symbolizing that He had come into His bride. Can you imagine the praise as He entered into the lower parts, the heart of the earth, like the heart of the woman, the one in which is between her legs. When He entered in there, can you imagine the praise of long-awaited saints who were held in captivity, who had died in the faith?

When He entered, there was a noise, a noise that the Savior had entered, a noise that the Redeemer was present, a noise that He had come to get His bride. And praise that came up from the heart of the earth, from the long-awaited saints was so tremendous, that called the hymen (veil) of the church to be red-torn.

Now all can enter. Why? Because truly Emanuel, God with us, is now God in us. The Christ now had come in to live with us. The anointed one had smeared, He had greeted us, He lubricated us with His precious holiness, that we had to open up and receive him. So it is with a woman. He anoints us with His oil until we are one with Him, until He penetrates us with His presence, with His love, with His Spirit, with His Word, with His heart, with His mind making us whole again. Because He brings with Himself no cancerous cells, but He brings with Himself life and with identity, we can be whole by knowing who we are and what He has done for us.

69

So great love, no greater love, that a man has than he lay his life down for his beloved, for his brethren, for his bride. That is why he said, "You really want a bride? Do you really want a bride?" The question is, are you really willing to die for her?

And He was willing to die for her that she might live, to enter in to her. So with that understanding, you enter into this place. The hymen is lubricated by thanksgiving, opened with praise, entrance prepared by lubrication, and anointing the veil is now open, entrance is ready, and now you go down the channels, the courts like the priests walking from the outer courts to the inner courts, into the holy of holies.

Remember; the priest brings with him the sprinklings all the way, because nobody wants dry praise. Dry praise is difficult, dry praise is painful, and dry praise is not receivable to the point one cannot open themselves up to dry praise. The priest comes in ready to give, not ready to take. He brings the offerings of the people, he brings sacrifice of the people, and he brings the sin of the people. But the offerings are greater than the sin. He brings the gift, he brings the fruit of life, he brings the sound of the bells of praise, because he must have the fruit of trustworthiness, the fruit of honesty, the fruit of integrity in order to enter in.

The priest enters in with the fruit that makes channels so much easier to receive and to walk in. The fruit clings against the sounds of thanksgiving, the sounds of holiness, the sounds of praise, the sound of love, the sound of treasure, the sound that say I am committed to you, the sounds that say I lay down my life for you. The sounds that say there is no one but you; come, go away with me to this place called bliss, called worship, where there are sounds of moaning or groaning that cannot be interpreted by anyone but the Holy One of Israel.

Only heart to heart, spirit to spirit understands such sound to what might others think it is foolish, the language of love. When mouth produces the sounds of the heart, one knows that they have entered into the holy of holies.

Let's go back a little bit farther. Let's take our studies we are talking about the healed woman—healing her softly. The female organs consist of external genitals. We understand that they are near the surface of the body between the thighs; they are protected, always between two—between the thighs, between the hips—like being between two guards that protect. They are also to open the external genitals inside the body; they connect one through another through the vagina and cervix of the uterus.

The external female organs are composed of the vulva and the vagina, surrounded by two major lips and two smaller lips. Between the two lips are the vulva and the entrance into the vagina. Notice that they are called lips; they are surrounded by the minor lips, which is called the clitoris. This is a small framed structure about the size of a pea. Just below it is the exit of the uterus, and this is so important, because this is where stimulation of women is hidden and composed. Notice that since it is outside, it must be stimulated prior to entering. It's like God. If there is no stimulation on the outside, there is no real penetration on the inside.

In my thinking, I think this is the reason why so many women are leaving the natural state of men; it is the ultimate satisfaction to be entered into, but the stimulation and the desire of wanting penetration comes from the clitoris, which is outside of the woman. She must be nurtured on the outside if we ever want to understand that the word always confirms itself. That is why the woman must be taken care of through housing, clothing, and trust. Proverbs 31 is so essential for her; it is apart of her.

The stimulation of the outside makes her want to open up on the inside. With that understanding, in this moment of pleasure, that stimulation is multifaceted, it is necessary to understand that because so many women are leaving the natural use of man because the stimulation of the outside must be satisfied so that the inside can come to full complete climatic organisms. That cannot happen unless understanding is given, to the clitoris of the outside. With that we understand that it is called lips, like the lips on the face must be stimulated or stroked so that desire of penetration is now compelling and nonresistant.

There is so much for us to learn in the body of Christ, so much to learn about sacredness of intimacy that we have to go to new depths and new heights. I think the reason why women turn to women is because women understand the stimulation on the outside--though it has a sense of fulfillment, it is not completely satisfied, because once satisfied there is a need for entrance that no other woman can fulfill. It can be satisfied and fulfilled only by a man. That is why we are having threesomes and twosomes. But all we need to have is a wholesome view of God and go back to the Author and the Finisher of the One that gave it in the beginning.

It is time for us to be healed by understanding these magnificent things that God called temples. If God calls us temples, then we must have an altar on the inside. The altar is placed so that all priests can reach it in order to truly offer a sacrifice. All priests must know how to enter the temple so that the praises be received and the burnt sacrifice can go up that ultimately a sweet aroma can be raised to the mighty God. It is time for us to be healed.

This healing is not by beating each other brains out in the bed, or hammering each other out, or coming out with the best freak show. It's by learning how to be priests that we know how to enter into the temple, into the presence, and come out with the best sacrifice one can come out with. Come out not with hatred, not with bitterness, but come out knowing that covenant has once again be reaffirmed and established and life has been released.

Part Five

I want to read the Amplified Bible as well as the King James Bible. We are coming from Genesis 3:16, which says something so powerful as to the fall of mankind: "Unto the woman he said, I will greatly multiply thy sorrow and thy conception; in sorrow thou shalt bring forth children; and thy desire shall be to thy husband, and he shall rule over thee." It is saying to the woman that now there is going to be multiplication or penetration with pain; there is going to be pain with child bearing—pain with producing that baby down with the channels of love came up. Love came up, child is coming out, pain now is going to accomplish it.

When a woman gets through having a baby after nine months, carrying life with her belly being stretched, back hurting, kidneys being pushed down, her uterus opens up, her water breaks, and the veil that had to break to let the penis in and now has to break to let the child out. With that understanding, now this pain can cause the average woman to close up and shut down because the pain is too great. Can you imagine her hymen broken by the head of the penis and now the head of a child coming through the uterus out through the same vagina where the penis entered?

Life was delivered on the altar, and now life is coming out. Now this woman has to remember the pain of having to push, the pain of being in labor, the pain of her water breaking, and sometimes the pain of difficulties of the baby having to be turned right side up, circumcisions, or vomiting, nausea for nine months. She can't sleep, having to walk or throwing up. And she could remember that all of this is the result of the act of having a sexual encounter with someone she loved. She could be forever turned off.

When God so wonderfully (outstanding, excites admiration and amazement, exceedingly pleasant) and fearfully made mankind that He allowed stimulation of the woman on the outside, long before the penetration on the inside, He gave that magnificent body a tool that she could be turned on, on the outside that would cause her to forget the pain she went through on the inside. Clitoris. If we could name the word of desire (wish for, want something very strongly), it would be that God gave the woman a clitoris. That no matter what kind of pain she went through, she could still be stimulated to desire her husband, to desire to be loved to be held.

According to science, the clitoris is very seldom diseased. It has no other function other than to stimulate or turn on. If we can understand how it operates by stimulation, by praise, by massaging, by nurturing, we can understand that even diseased women could be nurtured. Even diseased love can be nurtured because it is still intact. Even wombs, even pain, can be stimulated because you don't have to reach in to open her up. You just know how to stimulate her, enclose her, to want to open up, and to desire.

Part Six

Unlocking a woman's vagina is as easy or as possible as unlocking her heart. There is a door; there is an unlocking device. This device is really called thanksgiving. Appreciation, gentleness, consideration, and one of the biggest unlocking things for the woman's heart and vagina is sincerely, "I'm sorry," "I repent," and this will not happen again on this matter.

Can we see that? Can we understand that humans are made in the image of God? And what God needs is what we need. After all is said and done, we need to be like David and know how to pray Psalm 51. I need a new spirit, I need a new heart that will produce new actions. The vagina was made for taking action, and it is in every way a noun. Its excitement, its comfort, it likes hand, it likes tenderness. To love women is to love all women, including the vagina. Again, it likes to be touched and be in familiar with who cares for them; they are and they need to be satisfied. Women have to learn how to teach as well as receive for complete satisfaction.

If all our bodies could see you, every part of us, it would cry out with a out loud voice, "Hold me, touch me, love me, make time for me, be patient with me, and understand me." This does not mean I don't want you to become me; there is a hunger, a pain, and loneliness. And the place of detachment is almost unbearable—it makes one numb, broken, invisible, or shamed, when all we need is just to be really loved. The vagina changes, it moves with cares, with cries, and with hurt. The birth of not only a sexual door, but it is also a tunnel, a passage way that can hide a tiny child and produce the greatest man. It pulsates with a heartbeat.

Like the heart, the vagina is capable of sacrificing. The heart is able to forgive and repair itself, and so is the vagina. It can shape itself to let us in. It can expand itself to let us out. And it can close itself to keep from being hurt.

The heart between my legs. I think so much of us do not really understand the vein of love we are in. Therefore if we really knew that someone cared for us, we can come empowered by success by developing and executing production, repair, and healing. That is phenomenal. That cannot start outside of us; it must start within us. An anonymous person once wrote, "I know that I did not discuss this with you before that I have been sexually abused. I used to be weak, now I am strong. I used to be shy and now I am intelligent. I used to fall apart but now I am together. I used to find no interest in life, now I am interesting myself.

I used to find the need of no conversations and now I have the need of interacting with peers of my own that have given me the same thought and time as I have given." Let's have issues, but the issues are now part of the solution. I have and am willing to work to do whatever I can with all my might to prevent what happened to me from happening to you. And if it has happened to you, I am willing to use my repair to help you repair. What happened to myself and to so many other women can see through happening again; it has reminded me that in my rush to gain self-esteem and to recover I have really lost blessed tenderness of caring and being a hand of helping.

I lost my body too. I thought it was ugly and scared and marked. But now I see all of me is in need of repair. Here I go, hands held high, heart open wide to the repairer until I get all of me back. And then all will see He truly came to set me free. But I talk about my concerns.

When I hear my own heart, I discover my own potential helping others by my experiences, healing them by my love, walking with them day by day. The world is safer and the most stable place in respect.

We are learning to respect each other, and we celebrate each other: women that celebrate women, children that celebrate mothers, mothers that celebrate grandparents, grandparents that celebrate their daughters. Women's health is on the rise because we celebrate who we are. Women's sexuality is free because I know that God created desire within me. Women's empowerment is enriched because I know I can walk beside you. This is a marvelous day. This is a day of healing. I'm not a bottomless pit. I am bottomless well of possibilities.

You see, there are so many women with so many stories with so many experiences. Like so many women I have experienced them all. I have a piece of these women in my heart. I, as they all do, discovered the connection between each one so we understand, understanding completely with the capability that women really have for each other. I realize I understood my mother more than I wanted to. I understood my sister because I really learned to understand me. And that's what I needed. Most of all, I needed to understand me.

When I watched my daughter-in-law give birth to my grandson (quite by surprise, I not planned to be there), I thought I had to go out to the waiting room, but like the Transformers, the bed transformed into the stirrups. The doctor came in right in the room where we had sat and waited for the contractions to start. Everything was transformed. The whole room, the waiting room, the room where we were waiting became the delivery room.

I have never seen birth before. I was always asleep with mine, but I needed to be there for her, so   I held her hand and then she grasped and she pushed, legs up in the stirrups, pains and groaning, until I saw a tiny little head penetrating through her uterus. She pushed again with sounds that were down in the belly—my goodness!

It was beautiful. Every sound of groans and pushing life was near the door of entrance. I thought of birth as pure pain and torture, but standing there watching this, I saw something quite beautiful. The most beautiful thing I have ever seen! Down from the channels of heaven, the result of love was coming through the channels with every push, encouraging the mother with another pain. Push harder! I can't wait to see everybody's faces. She pushed again, and out came a hand. I saw the face unveil. One more push, and the shoulders are out.

Then the doctor had to be sure he caught the life that had come through the channels of eternity. The same way the priest had walked in and placed him on the altar with care, love, delight, and pleasure, now he comes out head first, making a noise. Bells were ringing to announce life. And what was birthed on the altar was named Keith. A child was given, a gift was handed, and the pain was now released. Love is something to see change come. I do not plan to change the world in a day, but perhaps in a lifetime day by day, blow by blow, until everyone understands that healing must be done with a soft hand.

Chapter 04

WOMANHOOD:
Second-Class Citizen or First-Class Daughter?

HEALINGHER
SOFTLY

Religion and Woman's Image

All too often, churches of today do not support women who strive to maintain an intact image. Many try to keep women "in their place." Or, as the old saying goes, "in the kitchen barefoot and pregnant." However, God has a lot to tell the world about women and men and how people should treat one another in all types of relationships. God has a lot to teach women about self-image as well.

Scriptures Teach Healthy Interpersonal Relationships

So often the Bible is used as a means of justifying the fact that women's images are being broken. Yet, if we study the scriptures, there are very clear directions about developing and living healthy, loving interpersonal relationships.
In Proverbs 18:22 God makes clear that a woman can be a wonderful blessing to the man who marries: "Whoso findeth a wife findeth a good thing, and obtaineth favour of the LORD." Again, God states that woman is a good thing and that it is God's intention that men and women have healthy, loving relationships.

God directs us to love and worship Him and also to love our neighbors. In Luke 10:27 we are all directed, both male and female to "love the Lord thy God with all thy heart, and with all thy soul, and with all thy strength, and with all thy mind; and thy neighbour as thyself." This clear message, if followed with consistency, would alleviate most of the world's problems, including those of women's images.

God wants everyone to be saved, and He wants us to pray for everyone. It is made quite clear that everyone, men and women, can lead a tranquil and quiet life in godliness and dignity by following God's directions: "I exhort therefore, that, first of all, supplications, prayers, intercessions, and giving of thanks, be made for all men; for kings, and for all that are in authority; that we may lead a quiet and peaceable life in all godliness and honesty.

For this is good and acceptable in the sight of God our Saviour; who will have all men to be saved, and to come unto the knowledge of the truth" (1 Tim. 2:1-4). There is no distinction between men and women when it comes to God's love. All human beings are loved by God; however, God hates sin and does not love our sin. But He is ready and waiting to forgive that sin when we come to Him through Jesus Christ, His Son.

The apostle Paul wrote in 1 Corinthians 11:11-12, "Nevertheless neither is the man without the woman, neither the woman without the man, in the Lord. For as the woman is of the man, even so is the man also by the woman; but all things of God." This passage of Scripture makes it clear that men and women need one another. Their lives are intertwined. God, however, needs to be part of each and every relationship of any kind.

Jesus loves women, even though they sin, and He is waiting to forgive those who love Him. The story of woman who washed Jesus' feet makes this quite clear:

And, behold, a woman in the city, which was a sinner, when she knew that Jesus sat at meat in the Pharisee's house, brought an alabaster box of ointment, and stood at his feet behind him weeping, and began to wash his feet with tears, and did wipe them with the hairs of her head, and kissed his feet, and anointed them with the ointment. Now when the Pharisee which had bidden him saw it, he spake within himself, saying, This man, if he were a prophet, would have known who and what manner of woman this is that toucheth him: for she is a sinner....And he turned to the woman, and said unto Simon, Seest thou this woman? I entered into thine house, thou gavest me no water for my feet: but she hath washed my feet with tears, and wiped them with the hairs of her head. Thou gavest me no kiss: but this woman since the time I came in hath not ceased to kiss my feet.....Wherefore I say unto thee, Her sins, which are many, are forgiven; for she loved much: but to whom little is forgiven, the same loveth little. And he said unto her, Thy sins are forgiven.... And he said to the woman, Thy faith hath saved thee; go in peace.

—Luke 7:37-39, 44-45, 47-48, 50

This woman who had sinned was not barred from God's forgiveness and love. Some people try to use this scripture to indicate that women should perform physical tasks for men; this is not the meaning. Jesus did not request anything be done for Him; this woman wanted to show her love and freely gave of her time, oil, tears, and love to minister to Jesus.

There are also many who tell women that they have no place in any type of ministry or service in the church. Yet Jesus traveled with and healed women frequently, as we see in Luke 8:1-3:

And it came to pass afterward, that he went throughout every city and village, preaching and shewing the glad tidings of the kingdom of God: and the twelve were with him, and certain women, which had been healed of evil spirits and infirmities, Mary called Magdalene, out of whom went seven devils, and Joanna the wife of Chuza Herod's steward, and Susanna, and many others, which ministered unto him of their substance.

In Jesus' time, it was forbidden for men to be near or to speak to another man's wife, much less befriend women and travel with them. Clearly, Jesus knew that God wanted women to be healed, loved, saved, and part of the church body—not as slaves or objects, but as servants of God. There are many other examples in the Bible of Jesus' sharing healthy fellowship with both men and women. After the crucifixion and resurrection, not only were women the first people to learn of this miracle; they were asked to do God's work by telling the disciples what had happened:

In the end of the sabbath, as it began to dawn toward the first day of the week, came Mary Magdalene and the other Mary to see the sepulchre. And, behold, there was a great earthquake: for the angel of the Lord descended from heaven, and came and rolled back the stone from the door, and sat upon it....And the angel answered and said unto the women, Fear not ye: for I know that ye seek Jesus, which was crucified. He is not here: for he is risen, as he said. Come, see the place where the Lord lay. And go quickly, and tell his disciples that he is risen from the dead; and, behold, he goeth before you into Galilee; there shall ye see him: lo, I have told you.

—Matthew 28:1-2, 5-7

Not only were women asked to perform God's work, but they were also visited by the resurrected Son of God soon after:

> And they departed quickly from the sepulcher with fear and great joy; and did run to bring his disciples word. And as they went to tell his disciples, behold, Jesus met them, saying, All hail. And they came and held him by the feet, and worshipped him. Then said Jesus unto them, Be not afraid: go tell my brethren that they go into Galilee, and there shall they see me.

> —Matthew 28:8-10

These women, after seeing their Jesus in His glorified body, were entrusted with very important information to delivery for Him.

The Issue of Submission

Much has been said about wives submitting to their husbands—usually to extremes. Look at what the apostle

Wives, submit yourselves unto your own husbands, as unto the Lord. For the husband is the head of the wife, even as Christ is the head of the church: and he is the saviour of the body. Therefore as the church is subject unto Christ, so let the wives be to their own husbands in every thing. Husbands, love your wives, even as Christ also loved the church, and gave himself for it; that he might sanctify and cleanse it with the washing of water by the word, that he might present it to himself a glorious church, not having spot, or wrinkle, or any such thing; but that it should be holy and without blemish. So ought men to love their wives as their own bodies. He that loveth his wife loveth himself.For no man ever yet hated his own flesh; but nourisheth and cherisheth it, even as the Lord the church: For we are members of his body, of his flesh, and of his bones.

For this cause shall a man leave his father and mother, and shall be joined unto his wife, and they two shall be one flesh. This is a great mystery: but I speak concerning Christ and the church. Nevertheless let every one of you in particular so love his wife even as himself; and the wife see that she reverence her husband.

—Ephesians 5:22-33

To sum up this Scripture passage: Each husband is to love his wife as himself, and the wife is to respect her husband.

- Man is to love woman and woman is to love man. Two bodies become one, the man being the head and the wife the body. This refers to the church, not to subservience. It does mean that women should submit to the man, and that the man should submit to God and love is wife as his own body. This is passage is sometimes used to keep women "in their place."

- The wife is to be subject to her husband in everything, and he is to sacrifice himself for her. The theme here is she submits, he sacrifices.

- The wife is the body, and the husband is the head. Together they form one flesh.

- The wife is to respect her husband, and the husband is to love his wife.

The Broken Image

It is easy to see why women become conflicted and do not know how to resolve their broken image. A woman with a broken image often feels her dreams cannot become reality. Because society and religion send one set of messages, while the Bible and her inner self send an entirely different set of messages, self-confidence and self-love break down, and she may begin living in one of the molds set for her by society and religion.

It should be noted that religion, in the meaning used above, does not refer to a personal relationship with God or salvation. It refers to man-made religion with its resultant legalism rather than true spirituality and a relationship with God. Only when a woman has a close personal relationship with God can these obstacles be overcome.

A God-fearing, God-loving husband and a loving family can provide the support needed to help the woman repair her broken image. God can heal all things, including a woman's broken image of herself—as we will see in the following chapters.

Chapter 05

One Broken Girl, One Flawed Woman

HEALINGHER
SOFTLY

This is a story about a little girl thrown into womanhood before her time. How many of us can identify with this little girl? For example: abandoned by Daddy, abused by an uncle, beaten by brothers, and called names by her cousins. In one flash of a moment, she is no longer a little Barbie doll sitting on the shelf ready to be dressed and played with. She is now a torn and worn thing in need of a tender touch—hurting, embarrassed, and ashamed, all the while not knowing whether her womanhood should be celebrated, ignored, or hated. Can you see this little girl suffering? Is it you? Lost, traumatized, abandoned, and hated—and needing to be healed softly.

Both you and I are that little girl, a little girl who was once shackled, longing to be free of the pain of being bounced from place to place and thrown around like a discarded rag. In her mind she is wondering, "Where is my place in life? Will I ever find trust and love again?" Let's journey through life's pages of pain, hurt, and despair to the place of being cured and healed. Let me share with you what God did for me.

Interestingly, quite by accident (actually, by God's intervention), I realized at thirty years of age that I was still suffering from the pains incurred at age four. No one had ever let me know that I could be healed of my past, but then again, maybe I never asked, thinking it was an impossible task anyway. You know how we women are: we tolerate, put up with, and endure because we are built to handle pain, although we often carry more than we should. It is amazing how God built us in such a way that as small as a uterus is, it can be stretched to the point that a baby comes out of it head first.

Yet we get over the pain as well as the experience of being stretched beyond measure for nine months. All women, even those who have not given birth, have been stretched beyond their limit—or what they thought was their limit—in some area of their lives.

All that I went through, witnessed, or observed should have just been a part of my life experiences, like a baby's head passing through a uterus, not an entire life of pain. The thirteen-year-old girl who was so afraid of being abandoned and left alone was trapped inside of a thirty-year-old woman. This same little girl, caged in the body of a woman now older in years, needed to be accepted and passionately loved, yet years of hurt had left her afraid of being abandoned, lonely, and unloved. They had left me without what I want the most—LOVE. It's funny, but I became afraid of what I wanted and needed the most.

I can never forget the little girl who slipped and fell in the blood of another woman—my neighbor. The horror of a woman shot by her own daughter was a nightmare that no one should experience.

The younger shot the older, the daughter shot the mother, and the third generation witnessed mother shooting grandmother. Micah 7:6 says:

> For the son dishonoreth the father, the daughter riseth up against her mother, the daughter in law against her mother in law; a man's enemies are the men of his own house.

Somehow that scene triggered in me fear and mistrust of women, as well as self-hatred. I came away from it believing that women are not persons to receive from but individuals to stay clear of.

Because of that, Titus chapter 2, which says that the older women are to teach the younger women how to love and take care of their husbands, children, and homes, could not come to pass in my life.

I will always remember that day very clearly—the smell of blood, the sight of which looked like red paint spilling over the floor; screaming and crying women; the aroma of gun smoke filling the air. I remember that day, even to the point of reliving it sometimes—people running to see a woman lying in a pool of her own blood as one daughter held the gun, the other daughter screamed, and I slipped, falling in the blood of the grandmother.

That moment seemed to initiate a series of constant falls in my life. This was the beginning of an invisible block holding me back, as well as a cloud hanging over my head, as the fear of being alone, in addition to a greater fear of distrusting women, was birthed and took hold of my life.

I wonder how many of us, like myself, have slipped down in another woman's blood and never gotten up. Maybe in your case it was not the blood of a neighbor, but the blood of a mother, a lover, a father, or a girlfriend who betrayed you; maybe the person who was supposed to heal you instead hurt you and left you to die. Maybe it was the blood of your husband, and it bled all over you, and now you think that men are no good. Maybe it was the blood of your grandmother that taught you that men are dogs. Was it the blood of a friend who told you about her abortion that left her bleeding on the bed? Was it the blood of your sister as you watched her die of AIDS and a broken heart? Whose blood did you slip in?

Are we all slipping in the blood of someone else? Now is the time that we stop slipping in the blood of others and our own blood and become washed by the blood of Jesus Christ. I had to realize that the blood I slipped in was a counterfeit to cause me to fear and even hate the precious blood of Jesus that could heal and take away my pain, even the pain in my heart and memories sustained at that early age that were trying to set up roadblocks to my salvation.

As I mentioned above, according to the Bible, the older women should be teaching the younger women while making them healthy, whole, restorers, mothers, wives, keepers of homes, and wise:

> The aged women likewise, that they be in behavior as becometh holiness, not false accusers, not given to much wine, teachers of good things; that they may teach the young women to be sober, to love their husbands, to love their children, to be discreet, chaste, keepers at home, good, obedient to their own husbands, that the word of God be not blasphemed.
>
> —Titus 2:3-5

Today the young women are taking the older women's husbands while the older women are full of disappointment and becoming bitter, angry, overweight by taking comfort in food, and disillusioned—while at the same time being religious.

They become angry with their silent God because them blame Him for killing, not healing; breaking, not restoring; destroying, not renewing. In their minds, He left them alone to raise children, to take of aging parents, to be grandparents, and to rock babies. Of course, they do not mind all this; in fact, they love it. It fills a void of safe love.

Those who rest and feed on our breasts will not hurt. But as we love, we also need to be loved. We need to be loved by our men, but I have learned and am still learning that we must be on the path of healing to receive love. We have to make room in our heart by asking the Holy Spirit to empty out everything that is amiss and then allow Him to fill them with His healing love.

Affirmation of my womanhood comes from another woman, particularly an older woman. When we dress, we often look for approval from another woman—or from the green-eyed monster that says "I have it." It becomes so important to tell a sister that she looks nice or help her to look nice. When we do that for each other, then we do not have to look for approval from men.

Now, I know there are times we all want to look desirable for the man in our life, but not for all men. Something is wrong when we want to become a sex object for all men; we really want more than a one-night stand.

Women need affirmation from both sexes, because older women teach us how to be transformed from a girl to a woman, and then from a woman to a lady, a wife, a lover, and a mother. Older women also teach younger women to cook, care for a house (including a husband and children), and, moreover, to love ourselves. So by the time we receive a husband, we have been taught how to keep ourselves and him as well as our homes by all the teachers who have been in place teaching us all along. We are ready and trained to be the lady friend and lover, the person he is proud to have on his arm and a pleasure to talk to as a friend and the one to take him to glory land.

I think the greatest need of churches is parenting, the parenting of both fathers and mothers. With the loss of the two-parent household, we lost the skills and effects of dual parenting. Somehow God always knew that an "US" had to make "them,"

> And God said, Let us make man in our own image, after our likeness: and let them have dominion over the fish of the sea, over the fowl of the air, and over the cattle, and over all the earth, and over every creeping thing that creepeth upon the earth.
>
> —Genesis 1:26

It takes two people to make a baby—one having the egg, the other having the sperm. It takes a man to develop a son, but it takes a woman to carry that son. A woman trains a daughter, and a husband now takes a wife, while a wife takes a husband as the two combined train a child, which makes them parents. The wonderful writing of Paul in Ephesians 5 compares our own households to the church itself. The two-parent household what heals our lives. We in the church always want a double blessing or double portion; what greater blessing could there be than a child who has the blessings of the mother and the authority of the father? This is symbolic of the two rains coming together. The latter and the former rain came together, in which a baby was conceived and a child was born. Just as the two rains came together to conceive the child, the two rains still need to come together for healthy, well-loved, and favored children.

The invisible block that was holding me back had to go in order for me to be able to move on. It had to be removed by a new look into my own womanhood as well as into the womanhood of those around me.

Who I was as a woman had to be defined by the One who created them, the One who made both male and female. I needed to see myself as the woman He created me to be, not the woman I had become due to circumstances, situations, and disappointments in my home and in my life. I had to isolate the negative experiences in my life and realize that they were not the way of life for me or the natural way of life for others.   They were cancerous to my life and those around me. What really makes cancer so dangerous is that it begins to spread by eating the body; it eats the good blood cells, the tissue, the skin, and then the bones, devouring everything in its path. The apostle Paul wrote:

> But if you bite and devour one another, take heed that ye be not consumed one of another.
> —Galatians 5:15

The only thing that kills cancer is isolation and removal. That is what we must begin to tell ourselves to be healed. The cancerous situations that happened and produced hurt are abnormal, but I am normal. The situations should be isolated, but more significantly, they should not, and will not, isolate me from my happiness, soundness, and love of life in which I can have wholeness in addition to healing and a cure.

> Behold, I will bring it health and cure, and I will cure them, and will reveal unto them the abundance of peace and truth.
> —Jeremiah 33:6

Chapter 06

Reflections From Broken Mirrors

HEALINGHER
SOFTLY

Having seen that many women have a broken image of themselves, it's easy to understand why they often view themselves as flawed. Often, the mirror in which they see their lives reflected as a whole is broken as well. The woman with a broken image of herself tends to associate herself with men who are also broken, and the woman tries to fix them. She expects these men to become something they are not, to fit into her mold. Without realizing it, she is doing the same thing that society and religion has done to her.

Imagine taking a glass and breaking it. Then glue all the broken pieces back together again. The glass may look as if it is whole and right, but it is still broken, with cracks throughout. Now, hold that broken glass in front of your face and look through it into a mirror. What do you see? You see a distorted image of a woman, a broken image. This is very much like what happens when a woman with a broken image looks at herself. She sees a flawed woman.

Outside Validation

Because a woman with a broken image sees a flawed reflection of herself, she tries to make herself feel as if this image were right and good. To do this, she may seek relationships with other people to validate that she is good, beautiful, and valuable. She may seek the approval of men since they seem to be powerful and valued. However, a woman with a broken image will tend to find men who also have broken images and see flawed reflections of themselves. This is how women find themselves in broken relationships. It is, however, important to realize that it is not the people who are broken; it is the images society and religion place upon them and the flawed way they see themselves. The people are still those same creatures that God created in His own image and, therefore, are good.

Broken Relationships

When a woman seeks outside validation to ensure herself she is of value, and does this by associating with men and women who, just like her, see broken images of themselves, the relationship created will be unhappy and perhaps even toxic.

Women who have allowed society to tell them that they are subservient to men for so long that they have come to believe this lie often seek domineering men who "keep them in their place." Other women feel lucky to find any kind of man willing to be with them and therefore choose abusive, cheating, lying, stealing men who treat them as objects.

Even women's relationships with other women friends are impacted by the broken image they have of themselves. Those cracks viewed in the reflection in the mirror show through in every relationship, every interaction, each and every day of these women's lives.

Children's relationships with their parents who have broken images of themselves are just as unhealthy. The mother who is seeking outside validation for herself finds little time to spend with her children teaching them right from wrong. She is too busy trying to find happiness outside herself.

Women who have broken images feel a great need for approval. They feel an emptiness inside that nothing seems to fill and often turn to drugs and alcohol to fill this hole inside, but that doesn't solve the problem either.

Broken Value Systems

As a result of all this searching outside herself for validation of her beauty, value, and goodness, a woman eventually has her entire value system erode. Even if she were brought up by good and righteous parents, the confusion of society's and religion's messages and the broken relationships in which she involves herself begin to cause her knowledge of what is right and wrong to disappear.

The woman comes to feel that her only value is as an object of sex for men or as a worker to take care of men. She feels that unless she does as men tell her, she will lose what little value and power she believes she holds.

Things that, as a young woman, she would never have thought she would possibly do become the norm. The bright lights of the barroom become appealing. Her home becomes simply a place to eat, sleep, and change clothes. Her children miss her and need her, but she doesn't notice because she is so very busy running after the approval of others.

She finds herself making "friends," but something inside her knows that these are only fair-weather friends. These friends are there for the party and there for the food, drink, sex, and entertainment. They are not there because they value her as a person. They are not there to add depth to her life.
because she develops relationships with men who have broken images of themselves, these men come and go, never forming a deep bond with her. They seek sex, approval, and shelter, but they do not give anything in return. They too have broken images of themselves.

What Is the Solution?

Because these broken images and flawed reflections of woman come from society's pressure and religion's misinformation that women are secondary, subservient creations not equal to man, the only way these images and reflections can be changed is for woman to see herself as God intended her to be. God, having made woman in His own image, does not want her to be broken or flawed. He created her in His perfect image, which is beautiful, right, and completely good.

Societal pressures

Women must realize that society's view that women can't do certain jobs and that women do not deserve the same pay and benefits as men for the same work is completely incorrect. While it has long been illegal to discriminate based on gender, it continues to occur in subtle, covert ways that can't be proven as discrimination.

Over the years, women have begun to be accepted into more roles in society. But this change is very slow in coming, and even then, the compensation provided to women in their jobs is almost without exception less than that provided to men in the same jobs. Society makes excuses such as "The man has to support his family" or "The man has to make more money than his wife" as ways to justify this behavior. However, many women are supporting multiple children all by themselves. This excuse just doesn't make sense.

Society also justifies its behavior by telling women that they will not be happy doing a job that was traditionally held by men. They aren't strong enough, hard-working enough, or are too delicate to perform the work. Again, this just doesn't make sense.

Women must demand that society accept them as capable of performing jobs that they can do without regard to who has performed that work in the past. Some women may not be able to lift heavy loads; other women are perfectly capable of performing this task. Women are just as hard-working as men, and sometimes more so. After all, giving birth to a child certainly is not an easy job!

Long ago women were thought to be incompetent to vote in elections. That view has changed with laws granting women the vote, and eventually even society's opinion has changed. The same must happen in the workplace.

Society also treats women as objects in other ways. Topless clubs where women's bodies are exposed for men to leer at are simply a means of keeping women subservient to men by forcing women who are beautiful but have little education and few marketable skills to stay in that line of work.

These women have no other way to earn sufficient money to support themselves and their families. So, in order to get money from men, they enter these establishments and then take on the stigma associated with those who work in these awful places. Very few men are forced to lower themselves to this level in order to earn a decent living.

These are only a few ways society uses to hold women back and prevent them from becoming whole, productive, and happy members of a society of equals. Yet, God created woman as equal to man. Just as the three members of the Holy Trinity—the Father, the Son, and the Holy Ghost—are all separate but equal, women are separate but equal to men. It is a matter of forcing society to acknowledge this fact.

This pressure placed on women is nothing new. It has been going on since Bible times. In Old Testament times, women were considered unclean when having their menses. They had to stay in a separate tent and were not allowed to speak to men or be seen by men. During childbirth they were forced to be attended only by women. They had to cover their faces. While men were allowed to have many wives, a woman had only one husband, and infidelity was frequently punished by death. Women were bought and sold like merchandise in a store. Sons were considered good because they provided a means for the man to pass his name and lineage on, while daughters were simply something that required the father to provide a dowry upon marriage. Mixed messages on the part of society have been delivered to women for millennia.

Religious Pressure

Modern religion and churches also work to keep women in their place. It should be noted that there is a huge difference between religion and spirituality. Spirituality is the relationship between a human being and God through prayer, meditation, study of His Word, and performance of His will for our lives. Religion, on the other hand, is the practice of certain rituals based on the expectations and demands of humans. Spirituality is God-based while religion is man-based.

We all know humans are not perfect. We were all created in the perfect image of God Himself, but because of sin our perfection was removed. We make errors in judgment and action, and we commit sins. This, however, does not justify the purposeful manipulation of Scripture to place women in positions of subservience. Satan, however, uses the human desire for power and control to use men to control women. Never was it God's intention for women to be considered less than men.

Men frequently use the Bible to justify their superiority. The fact that Genesis states that man was created first is used by men to prove that men are better in God's sight. Eve's creation from Adam's rib is also used by men to place women in secondary positions.

Ephesians chapter 5 is a scripture frequently used to discount the value of women. Because the apostle Paul compares the church to a marriage, stating that two persons become one with the man representing the head and the woman representing the body, this text has been repeatedly used to justify keeping women "in their place." This is not at all what Paul intended. This was simply an illustration to help people understand how the church relates to Jesus Christ.

The church, instead of putting women down, should be providing counseling and support for women facing the challenges of today's society and religion. Some God-directed churches are doing just that, but far too many are not joining in this acknowledgment of women's equality.

By regarding women as second-rate citizens, the church implies that God created second-best creations. We know that God's creations are perfect and exactly as He intended them to be. (This is covered in more detail in chapter 3, "Womanhood: Second-Class Citizen or First-Class Daughter?")

Flawed Relationships

When women have a flawed idea of who they are and how they should relate to God and the people around them, they seek approval and self-worth from outside themselves. Because they see themselves through the cracked glass when looking in the mirror, they enter into relationships that are not healthy and good for them. This is because they use the same cracked glass when looking at those people they allow into their lives. As a result they select men with broken images and other women with broken images to include in their lives. The result is unhappiness, lack of fulfillment, and much pain.

The "in crowd"

At a very young age, girls with flawed images of themselves begin to seek approval from friends at school and those they meet in other ways. The "in crowd" is always considered the right crowd if a girl needs validation. Peer pressure begins.

The first opportunities to use tobacco, drugs, and alcohol usually arise out of these in crowd friendships. Frequently the young girl will enter into sexual relationships to be considered cool and acceptable. After all, the young girl justifies, the other girls are doing it. A pregnancy at an early age can result, as can sexually transmitted diseases, because it isn't cool to use protection. Abortion may be a choice the young girl makes, or she may choose to have a baby she is not prepared to care for properly.

The young girl often learns that to be popular, she must submit to whatever the boys in this group want from her. These flawed boys seek sex, validation of their immoral activities, and sometimes even making the young girl the object of abuse.

All the wrong men

As the young girl grows into a woman, she will most likely continue to follow this pattern of choosing the wrong men with which to form relationships. Instead of seeking out the man with whom God intended her to form a monogamous, life-long bond, she allows men to come and go from her life, leaving her feeling even more worthless and hopeless.

Domineering men

Some of the men she will encounter are domineering and demand that women be subservient to their every desire. These men want to control all the money to keep the woman from getting out of line. They want to be a sole focus of the relationship. Everything is about what they want and never about what the woman wants or needs. These men may, at first, seem to be perfect and caring, but over time their domineering comes to the forefront, taking over the relationship completely. These men live by the motto, "It's my way or the highway." Women stay with these men from fear of being alone or financial dependency.

Emotionally unavailable men

These men can appear to be a lot like domineering men because their view of life is that they are the center of the universe. The difference is that emotionally unavailable men do not provide emotionally satisfying bonding. They care about themselves and their jobs, but they are never there emotionally for their partner. When they have a crisis, they require support from the woman; on the other hand, when the woman has an emotional crisis, she has to rely solely on herself because the man will never provide support. Rarely, if ever, do these men express affection, and frequently they are incapable of even saying they care.

Women stay with this type of man because they feel they may not be able to find anyone better. Often, these men are good providers and can be workaholics, validating themselves through their careers but never having time for their partners.

Physically abusive men

Men who have never learned to handle disagreements properly often turn to physical force to get their way in a relationship. When angered, these men do not use normal and healthy outlets; instead, the rage builds up to a level where the stronger man takes it out on the woman physically. Too often these violent rages end in the woman's hospitalization or even death.

Women stay with these men out of desperation, low self-esteem, and fear. They have often allowed themselves to become financially dependent on them and see no way out. They fear that if they do try to leave, they will simply be hunted down and killed like an animal.

Verbally abusive men

Instead of taking their rage out physically, these men use words like knives to cut the woman to her heart. The woman begins to believe that the awful things the man says must be true. She is often verbally abused in front of other people, ensuring that her already low self-esteem is completely demolished.

These men have not learned to communicate effectively and to work things out through normal negotiation and compromise. They see verbal abuse as their only means of maintaining the upper hand. Women stay with these men because they believe inside that they are as bad as the verbally abusive men have said and that no one else would want them.

Unfaithful men

These men abuse the women in relationships with them by having sexual encounters with other women. They validate themselves and their manhood through multiple sexual partners. When the woman learns of the infidelity, the unfaithful man tells her that she isn't good enough to satisfy his needs. These complicated relationships can hurt many people, breaking more than one family apart.

Women stay with these men because they feel they need the man and love him. They do not have the confidence and esteem to realize that they do not have to tolerate this form of abuse. They feel they do not deserve a God-loving, respectful, and caring male partner in their lives.

Sexually abusive men

Men who are sexually abusive use sex as a weapon to hurt those who love them. These men do not care about their sexual partner's happiness or satisfaction; they only care that they get the kind of sex they want exactly when they want it.

These men demand their partners perform perverted sexual acts or have sex with other men while they watch. When their partner doesn't want to have sex, they threaten her with desertion or infidelity to get what they want.

Sexual abuse can take many forms. The following are some of them. The abuser has:

- Told anti-women jokes and/or made demeaning remarks about women (of a sexual nature)

- Treated women as sexual objects

- Gotten jealous, angry, and/or assumed you would like to or were having sex with any available man (or woman)

- Insisted that you dress in a more sexual way than you wanted or made demeaning remarks about how you dress

- Made demeaning remarks about your body and/or body parts

- Minimized your feelings about sex

- Berated you about your sexual history; blamed you if you were abused in the past or as a child

- Criticized you sexually; for example, called you frigid, etc.

- Called you a whore or a slut

- Withheld sexual affection

- Forced you to beg for sexual affection

- Forced you to strip when you did not want to, either alone or in the presence of others

- Openly showed sexual interest in other women when you were in public or at home; for example, while watching TV

- Had affairs with other women (often flauting them) after agreeing not to have sex with anyone but you

- Forced you to have sex with him
- Forced you to have sex with others
- Forced particular unwanted sexual acts
- Forced sex after battering
- Forced sex when you were sick or when it was a danger to your health
- Forced sex with the purpose of hurting you with objects or weapons
- Committed sadistic sexual acts
- Forced you to pose for sexual photographs
- Forced you to have sex with animals

Sexual abuse is not just forced intercourse. The above are some of the many forms that sexual abuse may take. They all demean and humiliate women, making them feel shameful and exposed.

The female partners of these men stay because they feel that they are worthless and have become so much of a sex object that they don't think anyone else would want them. They have come to believe, through society's pressures, that they are responsible for servicing their partner when and how he wishes.

Psychologically abusive men

Men who abuse women psychologically often use a combination of the abuses already discussed to manipulate and control women in their lives. These men make their partners believe that they can't live without the man and that they are worthless except as part of a relationship.

Women who stay with this type of man have bought into the manipulation and have come to accept that they are simply objects, worthless, and have a responsibility to do whatever the man wants. They believe that society will not accept them if they object and revolt. These women have so little self-esteem left that they truly do not feel they can become independent and survive alone.

Financially abusive men

Some men use money to control women. Single mothers struggling to survive are often attracted to the man with a broken image that seems, at first, to provide a solution and security. However, as the relationship develops, the man controls the finances, lowering already fragile self-esteem even further.

Frequently these men take the woman's paycheck on pay-day, and she is not even allowed to manage her own money, much less have any control or information about what he earns. Women stay with these men because they simply don't want to return to the struggle of attempting to survive alone or as a single mother. Because she has allowed the man to tell her for so long that she is not capable of managing money, she may well believe this. Because of low self-esteem, she is unlikely to secure a better job and escape the financial abuse.

Other broken men

Other types of broken men a woman with a broken image may encounter include the alcohol or drug addict, the sociopath who can't tell right from wrong, and the dangerous or criminal man. However, the most common type of other broken men that women meet are those that combine several aspects of the types of abuse above into their personality and behavior.

The Solution

The only way a woman with a broken image can repair her image nd begin to see herself as God sees her—perfect and whole—is to come to God for His healing mercy. We must go past the broken mirror and look at the Maker of the mirror. After placing trust in Jesus Christ and beginning a close walk with God, she can then—and only then—begin to heal her image of herself and make it whole again.

Because God has a plan for all of us, a plan that is much better and more satisfying than any plan we could develop ourselves, He will lead the woman with a healing vision of herself down pathways of abundance, happiness, joy, praise, and worship.

Chapter 07

Broken Girls Become Flawed Women

HEALINGHER
SOFTLY

What happens to the broken little girls as we mature and grow up to become women? What happens when we carry our brokenness with us through marriage, children, a new church, or job?

We must first understand that if we truly believe we were created in the image of God, then much of our so-called brokenness comes in the form of attacks by the enemy. He is so angry we aren't in his camp anymore. He wants to stop us from growing spiritually. He will do anything to keep us from celebrating our salvation and the abundant life God has for us. He wants us to be stuck in muck and stay there. He wants us to be broken and not believe we can ever be put back together again.

Let me take you back to the Bible and the children of Israel when God delivered them out of Egypt. Did you know God has already delivered you out of Egypt? You are saved! You are in your promised land. Believe it and live like it!

The process God was going to do in your life began while you were still in Egypt. He had to do it while you were still there, you understand, because if He couldn't begin in Egypt, then you would have never come out of Egypt. God wanted you to know that nothing that had you bound in Egypt could keep you in Egypt when He got ready for you to come out. Hallelujah! There was no lover that could keep you in Egypt, there was no habit that could keep you in Egypt, there was no attitude, no liquor, no crack, no cigarettes, no tobacco, no beer, no .45, nothing that could keep you in Egypt when He was ready to get you out!

God sent the blood to Egypt to fetch you out. You didn't do it yourself. Somebody prayed for you while you were lost in Egypt. You thought you made up your own mind, didn't you? You thought you got tired all by yourself? No! You thought you did it by your lonesome? No!

Somebody's prayers were mighty enough to carry the power of the blood right to you. Therefore you ought to always be faithful and pray, beloved, because somebody prayed for you. Be careful about getting attitudes in the body of Christ, because you don't know who prayed you out of Egypt.

You might have thought it was your momma and daddy; we hope it was, but it might not have been. You might have thought it was your brother, sister, or cousin, but you really don't know. It was some Moses who went down to Egypt, who had the power of God, the rod of God, the lamb of God, the calling of God, the anointing of God, and prayed, "Let my people go." Without that kind of direction, covering, and anointing, nothing would prevail.

On the way out of Egypt, do you remember how God instructed the Israelites to apply the blood? It was to be placed on the two sideposts and the upper doorpost to spare them from the angel of death. These posts are your body, which must be covered with the blood. Now God says, "It's not only good enough for the blood to be over you and around you.

You must eat it. You must drink it. Then after it's over you, around you, and in you, then it's time for you to walk in it and right through it." Now, let's make it personal: It's not good enough for the blood to be only over me and around me. I must eat it. I must drink it. Then after it's over me, around me, and in me, it's time for me to walk in it and right through it. It's a bloody pathway that leads from unrighteousness to righteousness.

You must make that transition from Egypt over to the Promised Land, because when you have the blood on you, around you and in you, it's dangerous to hang around Egypt.

So where are we as daughters in Christ? We are victorious because of the blood of the lamb! Hallelujah. And because of the blood God says, "Now that the blood is on you, in you, and around you, you can walk through anything, because there is nothing in death, hell, or the grave that can kill you now. I can cause you to walk right through the valley of the shadow of death, and nothing can hurt you. Understand, My sweet daughter, that what I kill, I can make rise again. But because the blood is on you, in you, and around you, I'm going carry you to the place that you fear the most. I'm going to carry you to rock-bottom. Everybody will give up on you, and you'll look like it's all over, but don't worry about it. You're just on the bottom of the ocean walking. Remember, I am there with you, and the blood is in you and around you."

Once we get over to the other side, when we make it over, our running days are done. The blood will take care of demons, pharaohs, and principalities. THIS IS THE GOOD NEWS! They can't follow you through the blood, so if they're after you, make sure you run to the Red Sea. And then when you get to the other side, REJOICE! SHOUT! And make a loud noise to God for the things He has brought you through! From the other side, you will see Pharaoh and all your enemies destroyed. Turn around, stand still, look at them, and watch them being destroyed!

Do we understand that the blood makes us righteous? And the blood destroys the enemy. This is critical for us to fully comprehend to live the life the Lord has called us to. Only the blood of Jesus makes us righteous; we are righteous by the covering of His blood. And this same blood destroys any power the enemy had over us in Egypt. For we have crossed over the Red Sea and are new creatures in Christ. All the enemy's bondage over us is gone. Our debt has been paid in full.

Now I found out in the body of Christ that even though the blood has taken care of the pharaohs, demons, and devils, there seems to be some things that leave for a season and then come right back again. This kind of baffles me. How can we come out of Egypt and then seem to keep one foot in the Promised Land and one foot in Egypt?

God wants to give us the power to turn those words off. Remember, "No weapon that is formed against thee shall prosper; and every tongue that shall rise against thee in judgment thou shalt condemn. This is the heritage of the servants of the Lord, and their righteousness is of me, saith the Lord" (Isa. 54:17). God will step in by giving us the power to turn those words and thoughts off so they cannot prosper against us.

This is our heritage! God wants us to know when we see these imaginations forming and the weapons forming, He's going to give us the power and maturity to be the discerner of thoughts and the very intent of the heart. This is not to put us in an attitude of fear, but so we might be aware and know how to protect ourselves from the enemy, be it a person in the body of Christ or whoever. What does God tell us to do with every high imagination, every thought, every tongue that rises against itself? He tells us to condemn it.

Part of our heritage is being able to stop negative words and thoughts that are formed against us. God says to not worry about the person who is thinking or saying evil about you or a particular situation; deal with your own thoughts and your own tongue. We don't have to receive what people are thinking or saying negatively about us, and we shouldn't!

This is the heritage of the servants of the Lord and their righteousness is of me, saith the Lord. [Reference??]

My sweet sister, are you allowing the enemy in the camp to create all sorts of wild imaginations to creep into your mind because of who you were before you met Jesus? Are you allowing what has happened to you in your past to slither across the Red Sea and attack you once again? Are you speaking negative words about yourself and your situation and believing them in your mind? Are you allowing what society says about who you were in Egypt affect who you are in Christ today?

Remember who you are in Christ! Remember you are a saint! You are a beloved child of God. You have been made righteous through the blood of Jesus, and no weapon formed against you will prosper. Don't allow the words of others or your own imagination rob you of all that God has for you to become. Don't allow the brokenness you now feel make you step out of the Promised Land and return to Egypt.

Chapter 08

Breaking Generational Curses

HEALINGHER
SOFTLY

What Is a Curse?

A curse can be defined as complications of life coming on a person because of sin and words of judgment coming from a person of relational or spiritual authority. This would include the following:

- Parents
- Husband or wife
- Legal guardian
- Spiritual authority figure
- God
- Yourself
- Occult practitioners
- Satanic influence

A curse can be a prayer for injury, harm, or misfortune to befall someone. Noah, for instance, pronounced a curse on Canaan (Gen. 9:25). Isaac pronounced a curse on anyone who cursed Jacob (Gen. 27:29).

In Bible times, a curse was considered to be more than a mere wishing that evil would befall one's enemies; it was believed to possess the power to bring about the evil the cursor spoke. Jesus taught Christians how to deal with curses:

> Bless them that curse you, and pray for them which
> despitefully use you.
> —Luke 6:28

Examples of Curses

In Deuteronomy 28, Moses lists the blessings and curses that will follow those who either obey the commandments of God or disobey them. Verses 1-14 give the blessings, and verses 15-68 list all the curses, some of which include:

- Poverty (v. 48)
- Business failures (vv. 20, 29)
- Troubled marriages (vv. 30, 56)
- Sickness (vv. 59, 61)
- Mental problems and emotional stress (vv. 28, 65-   67)
- Problem children (vv. 32, 41)

Exodus 34:6-7 and 20:5 states that God will visit the iniquity of the father on the children to the third and fourth generations—iniquities, judgment, penalty, and rebellion. Deuteronomy 23:2-3 tells us:

A bastard shall not enter into the congregation of the LORD; even to his tenth generation shall he not enter into the congregation of the LORD. An Ammonite or Moabite shall not enter into the congregation of the LORD; even to their tenth generation shall they not enter the congregation of the LORD for ever.

According to the dictionary, a generation can be defined as, a body of living beings constituting a single step in the line of descent from an ancestor; a group of individuals born and living contemporaneously. In other words, a generation is a single succession made up of a set of individuals who share a common ancestor in the line of descent. You can see this in the following scriptures:

And I will establish my covenant between me and thee and thy seed after thee in their generations for an everlasting covenant, to be a God unto thee, and to thy seed after thee.

—Genesis 17:7

And Joseph died, and all his brethren, and all that generation.

—Exodus 1:6

So all the generations from Abraham to David are fourteen generations; and from David until the carrying away into Babylon are fourteen generations; and from the carrying away into Babylon unto Christ are fourteen generations.

—Matthew 1:17

The word generation usually occurs when the Bible gives a genealogical or historical account of a family or tribe. The English understanding of generation is usually the average period of time between the birth of a parent and the birth of his firstborn child, usually about twenty-five to thirty years.

The chart below will show some of the people groups of the Bible and their generational lineage. It also gives scriptures to show some of the characteristics of the generational curses they experienced.

People Group	Characteristics	Scripture Reference
Moabites: an incestuous son of Lot; also his territory and his descendants	Idolatrous	1 Kings 11:7
	Wealth	Jeremiah 48:1-7
	Superstitious	Jeremiah 27:3-9
	Satisfied	Jeremiah 48:11
Ammonites: a patron in the sense of publicity, prominence; this, a mountaineer, an Emorite, one of the Canaanite tribes	Proud	Jeremiah 48:29
	Cruelty	Amos 1:13
	Pride	Zephaniah 2:9-10
	Callousness	Ezekiel 25:3, 6
	Idolatry	1 Kings 11:7, 33
Hittites: a people from the land of Canaan. The were one of the people who were driven out when Israel conquered Canaan under Joshua (Exod. 3:8, 17; Deut. 7:1; Judg. 3:5).		

And say, Thus saith the Lord GOD unto Jerusalem; Thy birth and thy nativity is of the land Canaan; thy father was an Amorite, and thy mother an Hittite.

—Ezekiel 16:3

A Curse Cannot Find a Place in Your Life
Unless There Is a Reason

The writer in Proverbs 26:2 states that there must be some basis in you for the curse to take root and harm or complicate your life:

- God: You knowingly disobey God's voice or Word and continue in sin—sexual immorality, unforgiveness, lying, not tithing, etc.

- Self-imposed: In Genesis 27:11-13 Rebekah called a curse on her self and never saw her son again. Some times we say things like "over my dead body" and then later reap the consequences.
  (Testimony of Ruth's legs and Wynn's twins.) You believe Satan's lies to your mind rather than what God says in His Word (for example,fear of cancer, divorce, and bad luck).

- Occult practitioner or satanic influence: Contact with the occult, such as we read in Deuteronomy 18:9-14; 7:25-26; Acts 19:18-20. In these passages we read about the Ephe sians, astrology, and good luck scroll—but then the Word of God grew.

How to Be Free—the 4 Rs

- Recognize: inner witness that this applies to you.

- Repent: repent for self and others, including friends and relatives.

- Renounce: renounce any particular curse, especially self - imposed, family, and/or satanic

- Resist: never accept what Satan plans for you.

Special Instructions for Breaking Generational Curses

If you are under attack from occult sources and someone has put a curse on you, it is indicative of the end time, as we read in 2 Timothy 3:8-13:

> Now as Jannes and Jambres withstood Moses, so do these also resist the truth: men of corrupt minds, reprobate concerning the faith. But they shall proceed no further: for their folly shall be manifest unto all men, as their's also was. But thou hast fully known my doctrine, manner of life, purpose, faith, longsuffering, charity, patience, persecutions, afflictions, which came unto me at Antioch, at Iconium, at Lystra; what persecutions I endured: but out of them all the Lord delivered me. Yea, and all that will live godly in Christ Jesus shall suffer persecution. But evil men and seducers shall wax worse and worse, deceiving, and being deceived.

But just as Moses and Paul did, we have authority over them:

> But Elymas the sorcerer (for so is his name by interpretation) withstood them, seeking to turn away the deputy from the faith. Then Saul, (who also is called Paul,) filled with the Holy Ghost, set his eyes on him, And said, O full of all subtilty and all mischief, thou child of the devil, thou enemy of all righteousness, wilt thou not cease to pervert the right ways of the Lord? And now, behold, the hand of the Lord is upon thee, and thou shalt be blind, not seeing the sun for a season. And immediately there fell on him a mist and a darkness; and he went about seeking some to lead him by the hand. Then the deputy, when he saw what was done, believed, being astonished at the doctrine of the Lord.
>
> —Acts 13:8-12

But in order to exercise our authority, we must put on the whole armor of God daily:

Wherefore take unto you the whole armour of God, that ye may be able to withstand in the evil day, and having done all, to stand. Stand therefore, having your loins girt about with truth, and having on the breastplate of righteousness; and your feet shod with the preparation of the gospel of peace; above all, taking the shield of faith, wherewith ye shall be able to quench all the fiery darts of the wicked. And take the helmet of salvation, and the sword of the Spirit, which is the word of God: praying always with all prayer and supplication in the Spirit, and watching thereunto with all perseverance and supplication for all saints;

—Ephesians 6:13-18

- The *shield of faith* will hide you and all that is behind it (Isa. 41:10- 12). According to Psalm 64:1-4, their darts are   words. In verses 7-8, God speaks one word and silences them. (Read also Daniel 7:21-22, 25 and Deuteronomy 23:5.)

- The *breastplate of righteousness.* Proverbs 4:23 says to watch over your heart with all your strength, for all the things there are in life come out of it. First Thessalonians 5:8 also tells us to put on the breastplate of faith and love. Faith works by love; stay loving and right with people. Don't give bitterness a home.

- The *sword of the Spirit*, which is the Word of God (Ps. 8:2, 149:5-9)

- All prayer and supplication in the Spirit, being watchful for the saints. Bind together in prayer; bind and loose; discern what may be trying to come. Be obedient to pray for one another as the Spirit leads.

Please understand that Satan cannot take your whole armor off; he just needs a little space to get poison through. For the purpose of a curse is to kill your temple. God in His infinite wisdom knew this and expressed His displeasure by the future destruction of Satan. God cursed him, and not only him, but also the dust of the ground that he was to eat the remaining day of his life. Subsequently, you must know that at no time did God curse man but rather chastised him (man) with sweat and pain, as for a prophecy of what Jesus would do in the Garden of Gethsemane identifying with man and accepting his own chastisement.

A Prayer for Deliverance and an Utter End to Curses

O Lord, the great and dreadful God, keeping the covenant and mercy to them that love him, and to them that keep his commandments; we have sinned, and have committed iniquity, and have done wickedly, and have rebelled, even by departing from thy precepts and from thy judgments: Neither have we hearkened unto thy servants the prophets, which spake in thy name to our kings, our princes, and our fathers, and to all the people of the land. O LORD, righteousness belongeth unto thee, but unto us confusion of faces, as at this day; to the men of Judah, and to the inhabitants of Jerusalem, and unto all Israel, that are near, and that are far off, through all the countries whither thou hast driven them, because of their trespass that they have trespassed against thee.

O Lord, to us belongeth confusion of face, to our kings, to our princes, and to our fathers, because we have sinned against thee. To the Lord our God belong mercies and forgivenesses, though we have rebelled against him; neither have we obeyed the voice of the LORD our God, to walk in his laws, which he set before us by his servants the prophets. Yea, all Israel have transgressed thy law, even by departing, that they might not obey thy voice; therefore the curse is poured upon us, and the oath that is written in the law of Moses the servant of God, because we have sinned against him. And he hath confirmed his words, which he spake against us, and against our judges that judged us, by bringing upon us a great evil: for under the whole heaven hath not been done as hath been done upon Jerusalem. As it is written in the law of Moses, all this evil is come upon us: yet made we not our prayer before the LORD our God, that we might turn from our iniquities, and understand thy truth. Therefore hath the LORD watched upon the evil, and brought it upon us: for the LORD our God is righteous in all his works which he doeth: for we obeyed not his voice. And now, O Lord our God, that hast brought thy people forth out of the land of Egypt with a mighty hand, and hast gotten thee renown, as at this day; we have sinned, we have done wickedly. O LORD, according to all thy righteousness, I beseech thee, let thine anger and thy fury be turned away from thy city Jerusalem, thy holy mountain: because for our sins, and for the iniquities of our fathers, Jerusalem and thy people are become a reproach to all that are about us.

Now therefore, O our God, hear the prayer of thy servant, and his supplications, and cause thy face to shine upon thy sanctuary that is desolate, for the Lord's sake. O my God, incline thine ear, and hear; open thine eyes, and behold our desolations, and the city which is called by thy name: for we do not present our supplications before thee for our righteousnesses, but for thy great mercies. O Lord, hear; O Lord, forgive; O Lord, hearken and do; defer not, for thine own sake, O my God: for thy city and thy people are called by thy name.

—Daniel 9:4-19

HEALING HER SOFTLY by Ann Evans

Chapter 09

Wholeness

HEALING HER SOFTLY

We have to analyze the type of relationships we want in life, ones that bring more disease or ones that bring cures. A cure helps to complete the healing process. According to Webster's New World Dictionary, cure is a systematic method that takes a particular course to make a total healing complete. It is a restoration remedy in which the elimination or total eradication of disease, distress, evil, and ailments takes place by which the open wounds are now closed. We understand that healing is not limited to one aspect of the triune being. When we experience being healed or cured, anywhere there is an ailment, disease, or despair, it is unlocked and then the mind, body, along with the soul can await refreshment.

Once we have begun the healing process, many times we desire to know our progress or status compared to where we were before. Often we measure it incorrectly. Our healing cannot be measured by numbers, degrees, or percentages. I cannot say that I am 50 percent or 90 percent healed. Neither can I measure myself by where others are, what they say, or what they think. When you constantly measure yourself by someone else, you will always be inferior, sick, and in need of something. Healing is measured by the amount of peace I have within myself as well as the peace I have for others. Real healing is the place where I can follow, flow, and be the best that I can be without injury to myself or others. It is where I can laugh and be laughed at. The laughter does not lead me into defeat or despair, but it propels me into my destiny. It is where I can live my life for myself with purpose, yet invite others to join me and help them to fulfill their life calling, purpose, and destiny. It is the place where I can now distinguish between what is healthy and unhealthy for me because I know the effects of my choices.   It is the place where I know what damages my own heart, mental health, soul, and life, so I am careful with what I bring into myself.

Phone 5.30

1. shea solutions deep
mositirizer

1. Pack wraps

1

3

$$\begin{array}{r} 2.88 \\ + 14 \\ \hline 3.02 \end{array}$$

) Quaker ~~Instant~~ Oatmeal 2.88 + ¢4

) Dial Soap 1.13 + ¢7 $\begin{array}{r} 1.13 \\ + .07 \\ \hline .20 \end{array}$

) Dial deodrant 1.08 + 1.08 + ¢ 0.14 $\begin{array}{r} 2 \\ 1.08 \\ 1.08 \\ + 14 \\ \hline 2.30 \end{array}$

) Soda's 74 × 4 $2.96

) bag Peanut butter graham cookies $1.07

) Softee Bergamot $1.73 + ¢ 0.10 $\begin{array}{r} 1.73 \\ + 0.10 \\ \hline 1.83 \end{array}$

() moon Pie ¢ 60

) Honey bun

	3.02
	1.20
18.28	2.30
$+\ \ 51$	2.96
18.79	1.07
	1.83
	0.60
	12.98
	$+\ 5.30$
	18.28

I am so glad that once Jesus begins the process of being healed, cured, and made whole, all limits that were previously on our lives, our beggar garments, are removed.

> And it came to pass, that as he was come nigh unto Jericho, a certain blind man sat by the way side begging.
> —Luke 18:35

What am I really getting myself into when I ask to be healed and cured? Being healed and cured now allows me to be in the position to be made whole.

DNA is God's signature or manufacturer seal placed on each of us showing that He was the creator. DNA is deoxyribonucleic acid, which is the chemical formula that makes us who we are. DNA is the mode by which things are passed from generation to generation.

DNA: Deoxyribonucleic acid. One of two types of molecules that encode genetic information. (The other is RNA. In humans DNA is the genetic material; RNA is transcribed from it. In some other organisms, RNA is the genetic material and, in reverse fashion, the DNA is transcribed from it.)

DNA is a double-stranded molecule held together by weak hydrogen bonds between base pairs of nucleotides. The molecule forms a double helix in which two strands of DNA spiral about one other. The double helix looks something like an immensely long ladder twisted into a helix, or coil. The sides of the "ladder" are formed by a backbone of sugar and phosphate molecules, and the "rungs" consist of nucleotide bases joined weakly in the middle by the hydrogen bonds.

There are four nucleotides in DNA. Each nucleotide contains a base: adenine (A), guanine (G), cytosine (C), or thymine (T). Base pairs form naturally only between A and T and between G and C so the base sequence of each single strand of DNA can be simply deduced from that of its partner strand.

The genetic code in DNA is in triplets such as ATG. The base sequence of that triplet in the partner strand is therefore TAC.

There is a specific design by which we were created that enables us to heal ourselves. God's plan was for us to have what we needed within to allow healing to flow throughout us and onto others. God never intended for hurt, pains, disappointment, and other things to stop His will, purpose, and plan for our lives. He equipped us from the very beginning to reach our destinies. For example, in a grape cell is the design for the vine, its preferred season for growth, and the flavor that enables you to differentiate it from pineapple, for example. In an apple cell is the blueprint for the apple tree, how it will look, taste, feel, when it will grow to be its best, and what will differentiate it from other things. The same is true for us; there is a blueprint for how we were made as well as the plan for our lives. Humans are so much more than clumps of tissues, so if the cell of a grapefruit contains all the capabilities of the entire tree, how much greater are our capabilities contained inside our cells and DNA.

There is a specific design by which we were created that enables us to heal ourselves. God's plan was for us to have what we needed within to allow healing to flow throughout us and onto others. God never intended for hurt, pains, disappointment, and other things to stop His will, purpose, and plan for our lives. He equipped us from the very beginning to reach our destinies. For example, in a grape cell is the design for the vine, its preferred season for growth, and the flavor that enables you to differentiate it from pineapple, for example. In an apple cell is the blueprint for the apple tree, how it will look, taste, feel, when it

Medicinenet.com
Definition of DNA, Medicinenet.com
http://www.medterms.com/script/main/art.asp?articlekey=3090

The same is true for us; there is a blueprint for how we were made as well as the plan for our lives. Humans are so much more than clumps of tissues, so if the cell of a grapefruit contains all the capabilities of the entire tree, how much greater are our capabilities contained inside our cells and DNA.

The human body represents a scientific revelation of the presence and personality of an Intelligent Designer of great wisdom who loves so much that he built healing into us. We are made up of cells, and within a single cell is where our healing dwells. We are designed with various ways to take action against injury and disease. When we get cut, every cell in that area begins to function according to its job description to bring healing to the affected area. We are a triune being; therefore, whatever occurs in the body will also occur in the spirit and soul. And though the representation of it will not be exactly the same, it will be comparable. The natural and the spiritual are mirrors of each other, so if a few cells can effect healing on a cut, then of course the spirit can also heal itself of wounds. Our design allows us to maintain ourselves through the innate mechanisms that are part of our makeup or DNA. This is the first gift God gave to us—the wisdom within our bodies to self-regulate for natural preservation and reestablishment of balance through wholeness in Christ, the root of our being.

Personal responsibility is the essential attribute of self-assisted healing. We have to take care of ourselves—all of ourselves, body, soul, and spirit, which includes heart, mind, as well as emotions. If our bodies are not in proper condition, then the cells will not be able to function correctly.

133

In order for healing to flow, we must total confidence it our restorative powers, but this requires wholeness in our spirit, soul, and body. According to Webster's New World Dictionary, whole is when something is uninjured, not broken, damaged or defective. Wholeness is when one is complete in oneself; the spirit, soul, and body are all in good health unified in strength. A state of wholeness means that God wants our entire being to be healthy and sound so we can be in a place to heal others while providing a way of escape, similar to the one provided for us.

The soul, body, and spirit are different but not separate entities. They are connected and greatly influence each other. Research shows that emotional pain excites the same parts of the brain as physical pain. So if your mind is in shambles, most likely your body will reflect the unstableness of your mind. Remember, they are all interconnected and they mirror each other, body, soul, and spirit. We have to seek the path to health and wholeness by making personal commitments to constantly take care of our hearts. We have to care for our entire being, taking in what is good for the spirit, the soul, and the body, realizing that one cannot work properly without the other. In whatever we do in our lives, we are constantly affecting our health, healing, and our eternity. Therefore, we have to really keep order and structure in our lives. God's plan for us is stated in His Word:

Beloved, I wish above all things that thou mayest prosper
and be in health even as thy soul prospereth.
—3 John 2

Medicinenet.com

The Lord has granted us three gifts of healing. The first gift is self-regulation. The second gift is the skill and understanding given to those in the medical and scientific fields to help us keep our bodies in the condition to self regulate. The third gift gives us the capacity for inner healing, set by the nature of our design, given by the Creator. The third gift will be our focus right now because we have to realign our inner self, which can assist in changing our overall well-being. Inner healing is healing of the heart, mind, and spirit, which is where most of the hurt and damage remains to live.

In Proverbs 17:22, inner healing is addressed: "A merry heart does good, like medicine, but a broken spirit dries up the bones" This means that a healed and strong inward being yields a healed and strong body.

Many of us have tried various things to obtain healing, some of which only made things worse. Much of our healing is blocked by our own doing, such as fear or negativity, which counteracts the healing process. Emotions and reactions are by-products to suffering, so fear and negativity could be running wild throughout many of our bodies. These emotions often have ill-effects on us that will increase our illness, if not completely surpass it by becoming an illness itself. Thoughts along with feelings can manipulate the body through the nervous system and the circulatory system. Since the brain is at the center of our nervous system, we really have to monitor what goes on in our minds. Mentally, you must seek to have "the mind of Christ" (1 Cor. 2:16) at all times, thereby remaining positive, hopeful, and joyful with grand feelings of thankfulness in all that you do or go through.

There also has to be balance in hearts as well as minds. We have to make sure our hearts continue to be purged. All unhealthy things must be pumped out on a regular basis and released while the healthy things are pumped in. Researchers are increasingly informing us of the role of depression, loneliness, unhappiness, fear, and anger in the development and prolongation of diseases such as cancer, heart disease, diabetes, and asthma.

We are physical, mental, and spiritual beings. We have to integrate all these aspects together to get a unified whole, which is greater than the sum of its parts. Our healing must take place in every part for us to receive a real life-changing healing that will thrust us onto the road to our destiny. We cannot fully operate as a complete being if one part of us is healed and other parts are still hurting or suffering pain. To prosper we must come back into conformity with the spiritual principles and precepts by which we were created.

Unification must begin to take place in us, which is the next step in the realignment process. After the inner self is realigned, the rest of our being has to be lined up and connected with the inner parts. Then the completeness of the entire person that mirrors the supernatural, ultimate triune being can now take effect. All of our human components have to be made one. This means that there is a balance as well as communication between the body, mind, emotions, and spirit, which are all now functioning properly. Research shows that the capacity of the levels at which our body is able to heal physically is directly connected to the wholeness along with the balance of mental and spiritual parts of our being.

James P. Gills, MD, *God's Prescription for Healing* (Lake Mary, FL: Siloam, 2004).

Physical health and healing refers to maintaining or reacquiring balance by adhering to guidelines that the body's design dictates. The guidelines are set forth in our DNA, which is our blueprint.

Having this balance allows us to tap into divine guidance. This is the only way we can truly be healthy and follow the Master as He guides us to our destiny. True divine guidance is the necessary element that allows the appropriate decisions that lead us in the direction of healing in every area of life, including food and lifestyle choices as well as human relationships. Our first accountability should be to the Word of God. Everything and everybody else need to line up behind that rock solid source of truth.

HEALING HER SOFTLY by Ann Evans

Chapter 10

Love Needs

HEALING HER
SOFTLY

As women, we understand that the things we are looking for are things that we want to feel. We are created emotionally that way. People, especially women, want to feel; they want to feel loved, and they want to know love. We understand that the feeling for the spiritual things is totally separate from the feeling for natural things.

I'm talking about emotional stability in marriage. While you may do some things repeatedly to appeal to your mate and please him to try to get his respect and acceptance of you, this error too often does nothing more than bring trouble to your marriage. We understand that when we discover our spouse's bad spots, we must carefully apply the balm of Gilead (healing oil) over them. We do not purpose to return them evil for evil, or use the knowledge we have obtained of their weaknesses to pull away or to deliberately hurt or irritate. We must learn to bathe those hurts in love and in the blood of Jesus Christ, learning how to lift those wounds up. Or as the wise man wrote: "For thou shalt heap coals of fire upon his head, and the LORD shall reward thee" (Proverbs 25:22).

We must learn to say, "Lord, this is where James is hurting, and this is where additional healing is needed. So, Father, I'm lifting him up in this area on the wings of love, and I am asking You to cover it by Your precious blood, for the blood will bring life and healing, that we may get on with our lives."
It's so important that we understand how to pray for each other's inner healing so that we can be in all ways whole and not be irritated by them. The more intimately you communicate with a person, the more mindful you need to be of that person and their feelings.

When you uncover a marriage partner's hurt, you need to handle yourself with caution and great care, and learn of your own needs and desires. Brush up on your understanding of the basic four emotional things that everybody needs. The four emotional gifts, or securities, are these: Everybody would like to be recognized, all people would like to be romanced at some point in their lives, and absolutely everyone needs to be loved and to have money. We all have these emotional needs, with no exceptions. Look for words to build up rather than tear down. Look for words that we can act on instead of react to. Look for words that will give excitement to your mate, that will cause him to want to see again. This way we can identify what motivates people to form a better understanding of each other. Human beings have fears and desires. We set up protective camouflage in words and actions for two reasons: protection, to keep others from knowing the true us; and to establish trust; only when we have come to trust each other will we openn our heart. Real reasons often lie deep down in some emotional valley: they must be carefully pulled up and looke at; but we are afraid to be exposed, and we certainly we don't want anyone else to see.

If you wish to get married and stay happily married, then your ability to control your emotions, the effect of your words and actions, is the greatest personal power from the Lord that you will ever gain. That's a big statement and a true statement!

Satisfying sexual relationships, for example, come only when we have met in the realm of our souls. Here, one partner's words or actions are satisfying to the other. Great sexual relationships in a marriage start with emotional reactions to communication in the living room and end up on fire in the bedroom!

Again, effective communication requires the proper emotional disposition—choosing to be sensitive to other people's feelings and to understand them, just like the Bible says. Secret fears or hesitation can harmfully affect physical relationships and produce abnormalities in everyone, especially women. Normal sexual cravings for complete intimacy and enjoyment in marital life is the heart and wish of every woman. Her actual experience, however, is sometimes so unsatisfying that her expectations become as routine as dusting the furniture. She begins to hate it because she doesn't know how to express or communicate the situation without damaging her partner; therefore, for whatever reason, her sexual life has become humdrum. Both she and her husband need romance. Both need to learn how to stoke the fires of romance in the marriage and the marriage bed, to bring excitement and the anticipation of something new and different—with the ones they have given their vows to!

One way you can do this is to learn how to make your own desires secondary. This is the greatest thing about a sexual relationship. Today, everybody becomes a taker—you know, "I want some," or "Give me some." The biggest thing about love is to give oneself. When we learn how to give ourself, we become completely satisfied; when we are only takers, we expect to be satisfied. When we learn to give all of ourself, we sow what we have reaped; then we find that our partner will learn how to give all of himself. Sexual satisfaction is not merely joining with an individual's body; it's when your body, soul, and spirit have come into oneness. Then the bride and the spirit say, "Come!" When we reach that place of openness, we go past the fears of being hurt.

When we touch that pinnacle and we're behind the veil, all we can do is cry out with tunes of harmony, because we are finally in the same place at the same time as God created us to be—one man andone woman. That's why He beckoned and tore the veil, so that the bride could come into the place of kindness, protection, love, mercy, and truth.

Remember the importance of listening: Proper emotions linking us together as we learn how to connect with each other in the living room. Let our hearts connect so that our joined bodies will achieve complete fulfillment and not roam.

Your own desires should become secondary as your ultimate goal is to fulfill and satisfy the needs of your mate. If each one approaches with the same idea—my goal is to satisfy my mate—then each will come in with the expectancy of satisfying rather than being satisfied. If both put all they receive from God into it, none will come out with anything less than desirable results.

Romance is a new experience for him and for her. It's days of unaccustomed warmth to be reached; it's harsh attitudes being smoothed away, which makes way for increasing burning desires. It's when passion is stimulated by kindness, reaching for my love and receiving with delight, not with suspicion. It's a new experience! It's not passively surrendering, making any excuse to just get it over with, but it's the communication of appreciation. After all, you still desire me. It's recognition that every person needs communication. And sexual relationships are communication relationships, too. They speak the highest, they shout the loudest, to bring us into a sphere of oneness, wholeness, and healing.

I so love the Word of God, for it says that the husband is to be the savior and healer of the body (Eph. 5:23). I cannot help but believe that. When true love is given, and real love is received, it can't do anything but heal! How often would our bodies be healed, and our marriages also, if we would practice the love that God has possessed us with, to share with one another, to put it into the preciousness and sacredness of marriage. For the blood covenant was absolutely established with the union of promises that speaks Yes to even our souls and bodies.

Love brings life, and life brings joy…with this understanding. We understand that one of the best places for us to be healed is in the sacredness, the fellowship, the arms, and the lovemaking of one another. I wonder how many marriages would be healed, how many bedrooms would produce miracles! Sexual relationship is a great communion; in response to love play, he becomes more imaginative and original in his arousing desires. This response eliminates the tedium of routine—hurry up and get it over with—that she has previously complained about or contemplated. All of a sudden now, her husband is a master lover; he's kinder and more considerate. Perhaps she has just had her first orgasm. The rewarding mutual relationship of communication, emotional healing, and insight is necessary, and they are so parallel to passion.

To gain such emotional insight you must be emotionally sensitive, not only to your needs but also to the needs of your partner. Sexual desire is romance, and satisfaction is really a kind of self-preservation. To achieve mutual fulfilling climaxes, both the physical and emotional realms must meet—delight bursts forth when words and actions begin to come together!

Such marital bliss and deep communication come from another world—heaven—where there is groaning and moaning that
cannot be absolutely understood; only the hearts of each other
that share them can approach understanding. Marriage is a state
of mind. When the mind focuses exclusively on its mate,when
the heart zeroes in on that which causes self-enclosed feelings to
be exposed—then we can successfully enter each other's heart
and mind to the place of trust. We come to the place where each
can penetrate the other's protective preoccupation and both can
now trust with their whole heart. In the book of Proverbs the
woman of virtue is absolutely commended by the Holy Spirit
and Solomon because the heart of her husband safely trusts in
her. Men are looking for a place where their heart can trust, because their heart is their dream, their life, their vision.

HEALING HER SOFTLY by Ann Evans

Chapter 11

Locked-up Love

HEALINGHER
SOFTLY

Women today have so many multiple roles that it is amazing that even perfectly adjusted, spiritually centered women survive! Sometimes it feels as if one more thing will just become too much to handle.

The Busy Woman

A woman who is a mother loves her children dearly and strives to fulfill their every need. This in itself can be a full-time job. That same woman may have a mate to care for and love, requiring time and energy. Her work outside the home is yet another full-time job. Her life is so filled with caring for others that there is little time to care for and love herself. It is not that she doesn't care for herself; there just isn't time in a day to do everything that is demanded of her.

Clearly, a woman needs time to treasure her body and her soul. She needs time to take care of her physical body. She also needs time to nurture her spirit and develop her relationship with God, her Maker. Her body and soul are sacrificed to allow her to meet all the other obligations of her life.

No matter how much money this woman earns, or how beautiful and healthy her children, or even how wonderful her mate, she finds that she is constantly pulled in too many directions. Her spirit becomes tattered and ragged. She carries burdens from her past, hurts she has never resolved, and issues she has never worked through because there is no time to worry about the past. She keeps on going day after day.

Somehow, this woman never finds personal and spiritual fulfillment no matter what she tries. Everyone wants some of her time, and she feels she simply must say Yes to every request. There is little joy and happiness in her life. She is surviving, but little else.

Time Pressure

Sometimes it feels like one more straw will simply break our backs. Too often, sleep and personal time suffer to satisfy the things that we feel we have to do. Too little time and too many chores and duties create a noise inside our heads that makes it all but impossible to relax.

The very act of looking at the clock and seeing the minutes of our lives tick away is one of the major causes of stress. We try to run faster and faster, getting nowhere.

Even our time away from work gets eaten up with duties. Children need to be given rides to activities to enrich their lives. Cars need maintenance. Homes need repair. It is a never-ending battle.

The Power of Saying No

We as women are taught at a very early age that we should please people by doing what they want us to do. We believe we are supposed to be the chairperson of the Parent-Teacher Association. We believe our children must have home-baked cookies. We buy into the idea that Yes is the only acceptable response to unacceptable requests for more of our time.

The only way to truly enrich our lives is to give ourselves permission to say no. There is no reason that a woman has to be everything to everybody. Sure, we want to be the best we can be, but by trying to be everything, we truly end up providing little quality love to those we truly care for.

When Less Is More

When a woman chooses to select carefully the activities she spends her valuable time on, she can make the time she needs to renew herself spiritually, physically, and emotionally. In fact, time seems to actually expand when we don't buy into society's idea that we must do it all. Setting aside time in the morning to commune with God can change the entire day. By taking time to read Scripture, pray, and meditate, our whole day can progress peacefully and calmly.

God wants us to pray, to talk to Him of our needs, our desires, our praise, and our thankfulness. God wants us to spend quite time meditating so that He can communicate to us. The psalmist makes this clear in Psalm 46:10: "Be still, and know that I am God." He doesn't shout at us. He speaks softly in the quiet times. Reading, studying, and memorizing scriptures reveals God's plan to us.

If we give less time to man and more time to God, there will seem to be more hours in the day, more peace in our hearts, and more joy in our souls. Everyone in our lives will find that we have plenty to give them of ourselves. All day, every day, trust God to provide time for those activities that are of true value and to provide strength to reject those activities that add nothing of value to our lives. Talk to God as a friend and He will direct the use of your time.

Ending the Time Battle

When a woman initially says No to duties and responsibilities that are not rightly hers, those around her will be shocked and surprised. Some people will act insulted; others will act with surprising support.   Slowly but surely a woman can, with God's help and direction, take control of her life and her time to do what God has in store for her. No one will suffer from turning time over to the control of God. After all, time—like everything else in the world—was created by God for the His glory and pleasure.

Gently but firmly explain to those who attempt to encroach on your time by placing unfair expectations upon you. If appropriate, explain that you simply have other duties that must be fulfilled. The rewards are worth the trouble of learning to practice the skill of saying No.

Rewards of Unlocking Love

The rewards given to who find the time to love those we care for are myriad. The peace and joy that are added to our lives alone makes it worthwhile. The energy saved can be given to truly valuable pursuits such as bonding with your family, both physically and spiritually. Getting up to go to church or other spiritually fulfilling events will no longer be a challenge. You will find more than enough time to do what really, truly matters.

Most of all, your children and mate will know that you have unlocked love because they will have the quality time with you they need so desperately. Children learn by example, and they can learn to lead peaceful, happy, relatively stress-free lives by learning how to unlock the love inside themselves. **Prison Book Project**

P.O. Box 1146
Sharpes, FL 32959

HEALING HER SOFTLY by Ann Evans

Chapter 12

Receiving Perfect Love From
Imperfect People

HEALING HER
SOFTLY

Everyone wants to be loved perfectly and unconditionally. It is a basic instinct of human nature. However, it is easy to believe that perfect love doesn't exist or that perfect love can only come from God because God is the only perfect thing in an imperfect world. Everyone God ever created sins and therefore is imperfect. So how can we enjoy perfect love when we are imperfect and when the people who love us are imperfect?

TYPES OF LOVE

Love doesn't come in only one form. Love doesn't just mean the emotion that is shared between a man and woman. There are five meanings for the word love. To learn the meanings for the types of love, we must study the five words for love in the Greek language.

Philia

Philia is the love between friends. This is the type of love you feel for your neighbors, best friends, social contacts, co-workers, and the stranger on the street. Scripture tells us to "love thy neighbor as thyself," meaning that we should have love for friends and others. This type of love adds depth and beauty to our lives. It causes us to share with others and provide charity to those less fortunate.

Storge

Storge is the love between family members. This is a love without sexual connotations, a love between brothers and sisters, mothers and children, fathers and children. This is the love that allows parent to love their children at all times even if they do not always love their children's actions.

Eros

Eros is the love shared between a man and woman. This is the love that creates the bond that allows children to be born; it is sexual love. This is where the word erotic comes from. This type of love is a very strong bond that, biblically, should never be broken. However, today's society tends to take eros love very lightly. This love does not refer to casual sexual activity, but it refers to the deep and abiding love that bonds two people of the opposite sex into a single entity.

Agape

Agape refers to the love of God for mankind. Like parental love, it allows God to love us even though He hates our sins. John 3:16 clearly defines agape: "For God so loved the world that he gave his only begotten Son, that whosoever believeth in him should not perish, but have everlasting life." This is, without a doubt, the only truly unconditional love in the universe. Many types of love can end because of our doing something bad. God's love goes on and on forever without exception. God even loves the worst sinners and wants to save them from eternal damnation.

Epithumia

This type of love is not really love but lust and desire for things. It can be all-consuming, blocking out all types of true love. It includes lust, impulse, and earnest desire for things and objects that we believe will make us happy.

The love of objects causes us to love without gaining any love in return. We give but do not receive love. Sometimes this type of love has a practical purpose. For example, a crumb of this love, such as a compliment on a bad day, can help us survive and hold up until our day improves. However, this type of love can often become an obsession.

This love can cause a lot of grief because objects can be lost. Beauty goes away with age in many cases. This love is ephemeral in nature.

Perfect Love From the Imperfect

Now that we understand the different types of love, let's look at how we receive perfect love from imperfect people. Let's look at how we can love perfectly even though we are imperfect.

Perfect philia

Have you ever had a friend who loved you dearly and you loved her dearly, yet at some time something bad happened between the two of you? I'm sure you have; everyone has these experiences. Did you later make up and again spend time together?

No earthly friend can ever be perfect. We will do things that are wrong, and sometimes those things can hurt even our dearest friend. You, even though you may be redeemed by God, are not perfect, and perhaps you have done something that hurt your friend. Does this mean that the love shared between two friends is imperfect? Is it bad? Should you not care for friends with love?

God created philia love. All that God created is good and perfect. Sin enters our lives and causes us to sin, which is an imperfect action. But it does not make the sinner less than God intended. God can and does help us love imperfect people with perfect love. He teaches us how to forgive by having forgiven us of our many sins, no matter how large or small those sins may be.

Using the example of God and Jesus' death on the cross, we must learn to forgive those who love in a philia way when they are less than perfect. This same example allows those friends to love us when we do something wrong inside the relationship. Forgiveness is a great gift that God has provided for us to be able to love perfectly those imperfect friends that fill our lives.

Perfect storge

If you are a parent, you probably understand the concept of perfect storge love. After giving birth to a beautiful, tiny child, your love is without depth or end. That child may do wrong things, break your favorite vase, wreck the car, or worse. But your love for that child goes on. You may hate some of the actions of that child, but you will never stop loving the child.

Again, this is an example of how God loves us. No matter what the child does, love doesn't stop. God's love for us imperfect humans doesn't end either. Parents sacrifice for children; God sacrificed His Son for us.
If there were no storge love, parents the world over would abandon children because of their bad actions. But only a very, very bad or severely mentally ill parent would ever abandon their child.

Perfect eros

When a man and woman fall in love, they experience eros, or erotic love. They create a bond. If this couple is God-centered, they can create a perfect bond even though both members of the couple are imperfect. This love allows the bond that will create a loving family for raising children with storge love.

At times during any marriage, the husband or wife does something that the other objects to strongly. Both of these humans are imperfect people, and no marriage is without any strife or disagreement. However, eros love allows that couple to love each other without allowing their problems, however large or small, to end the family and cause them to stop loving each other.

Perfect eros is the type of love that we see in a couple who, after decades together, still love each other, hold hands, kiss, and share a special bond between themselves.

Perfect agape

God's love for us is perfect by its very nature. However, all too often, we humans choose not to receive this love. God never stops loving perfectly; we simply move away from this perfect love.

Agape is the only love that is perfect without our having to earn it. We did nothing to earn this love. It is not dependent on how pretty we are, how smart we are, or any other factor in our control. It is not based on the position in society to which we are born, nor is it based on the amount of money we have. It is always flowing from heaven to our hearts.

We simply have to accept this perfect love to enjoy all the benefits of agape love. God's Son died to redeem us, but even while we live in sin, God loves us perfectly.

HEALING HER SOFTLY by Ann Evans

Chapter 13

THE LANGUAGE OF LOVE

HEALINGHER
SOFTLY

There is a language of the heart that is deeper than any other language; it's called the language of love. This is what every creature under heaven knows and is familiar with. Even the birds and the bees have a mating season. All have a season of love, and man is no different. For the creator of man is known as love. That's right, God Himself is known as love. This God we have, we share, and we know does everything out of the need of expressing, desiring, and wanting love. As His creatures and creations made in His image, we desire no less than our God desires. We also desire praise, and we have a vacuum just to be loved.

Women are mesmerized by love. Everything they do is out of the need for love, to feel love, to give love, and to express love. As women, we must know that God loves us. We must know that in our relationships we are loved. No matter what, the bottom line is I must know that God loves me, no matter what or who walks away from me, who stays with me, who finds me attractive or unattractive, or sexy or not sexy, or intelligent or not so intelligent. We must come to a resolution in our hearts that God, El Shaddai, the one who promised He would be there, will always be there for me. That is the only way we can make it.

We can no longer live in the fear of abandonment, of being alone, or of rejection. We have to know that God has accepted us into the beloved, no matter what religion says, men say, or we ourselves sometimes think. God loves me—woman, man with a womb—and His plans for me are also just as great at His plans for Adam. God has a plan for my life and feels deeply about me. God deeply loves me. I must feel and know that God deeply loves me; likewise I must love and accept myself as a primary thought and not a secondary thought.

The nature of love itself is a giver, and a giver must have a receiver. God built us to receive love. Love is not a solo experience, but requires both a giver and a receiver, a lover and a responder to love.

If our culture says God is harsh, judgmental, prejudiced, and not a respecter of persons, then we tend to pursue accordingly with fear, with doubt, and certainly not with trust. Love is a matter of the heart, love is the renewal of the soul, and love is the illumination of the spirit. We must be convinced of God's love and know His primary language of love. God loves us; He speaks love language and knows what love language you need to hear. That is why on the Day of Pentecost, all heard the Spirit that comes to share the breath and the love of God in their own language. The love language—women love all that concerns love. They love everything about love. They love the idea of being in love, they love being in love, they love being loved. It is the love language.

We all know that children need the love language; they need to feel loved. Regardless of how sincere parents must be, the key is knowing the love language and how to express it. The primary language of a child, of a baby, is speaking readily, "I love you." The kissing, the hugs, the holds, the rocks, the cues, the words—even though the child may not apprehend the language, it apprehends the expression, the touch, the care. And that is the same way we must make each other feel in husband and wife relationships. We must make each other feel loved. The need for love, unexpressed, causes one to feel unfulfilled. We understand and know what to do so many times; we just don't want to do it or, perhaps we think those things are unnecessary.

People who choose not to love, or who are never happy people, or who choose not to express it, or who are closed in people—that lack of love not only hurts the other person, but it also causes the one that could give it to miss out on the greatest gift that man has ever been given under the sun next to God: the ability to receive love and give love. This is what I tell my couples when they come in to see me for counseling.

You understand that you have the greatest opportunity to apprehend the greatest miracle in the world—to love and to be loved. People who refuse to love live on the edge of desperation, just tired of living and tired of living alone as well as scared of dying and dying alone. Life without love is the greatest death of all. Life is more effective when you learn to love each other and enjoy the joy of living and the peace of dying with someone who loves you. To love and to be loved, Lord, is the need of all human beings. Very few things are more important than that. It is not something that you can buy. You can buy an imitation of it, but you cannot buy the real thing.

Love is tapping into divine love. The author, the finisher, the creator and love itself is really divine, and that is what God is—Jehovah Shammah [I am not familiar with this term-J. Dennis]. He is really love, and God loves to love. He knows our heart language; our heart language of love must be spoken, expressed, and manifested, so we the creatures created in the image of God, His children—moreover, His bride—will understand the language of love. We expect Him to love us, we expect others to love us, and we expect the love we give to be reciprocated.

This is illustrated in every relationship under the sun: parent and child, family and friends, congregation and pastor, and most of all, husbands and wives. A child is a creation of parents, and this child needs love from both parents. Neither one of them can do the job completely or perfectly without the other. We realize that in our society it is being done, and we salute those who are trying so very desperately to make up for two-parent love singly. In loving our children, we form an emotional and spiritual bonding with them, just as we do with God,. We are willing to give much of ourselves in exchange for the happiness of other lives; this is what love does. This is what God did in the giving of His Son, Jesus Christ, for us.

I believe parental love is a reflection of divine love called storge, a strong love that is there no matter what. I can go through the hardest, roughest time and yet not give up or give in. God's love for mankind and His parental love is so much like storge. We can't expect a natural, ungodly man to be capable of responding to God's kind of love. He can make that response only by means of a love connection with God Himself as he responds to the love of God. If a man understands himself to be truly in the image of God, he will be able to connect with his God so that he may carry out the human desire that craves a father's love. All children crave a father's love. All children crave the love not only of the mother but the love of the father as well. The need to be loved brings about security, happiness, and fulfillment in one's life. Children are an example of this. To know God is to be loved by God, to be connected with God; for without God's love one cannot reflect the love of God, the nature of God, the heart of God, the person of God. God is love, and love is God.

We should never underestimate what God created: creatures capable of love, creatres that He can enter into and become one with Him. If we understand the dynamics of human love, it will help us with the expression of divine love. Unfortunately, very often love is not highly regarded because so often the love language has been misappropriated and thus misinterpreted. There are five basic love languages, and certainly we give tribute to Gary Chapman for his best-selling book The Five Languages of Love. We also want to say that there are five types of love. When one speaks another's primary love language, it that one is fulfilling a basic need of another to feel loved. When a person does not speak my primary language I wonder whether he or she really loves me. Emotionally I am not understanding that person. I do not understand a person who does not speak my language when I am doing everything I can to speak theirs.

The problem within many human relationships is that you and I speak our own love language, and sometimes we do not understand our partner's love language. We are speaking our own language and wonder why our partner does not understand.

He may be speaking a love language, but it is not ours. It is like a person who speaks Spanish and I speak English. Yes, we are communicating, but the communication is not on the same page; the sequence is wrong. We must understand what is being given so we can receive, and what is being received so we can properly respond. Human relationships are enhanced when we learn to speak each other's personal love language.

The love language that women need are words of affirmation. Affirmation is a big deal with women; it is constantly, "Do you think I am pretty?" "Do you think I am attractive?" "Do you think I am sexy?" "How was the meal?" "How do you like the house,the dress,the gift I bought?" "Do you like my hair?" Women are constantly looking for words of affirmation,words that let her know that she is loved and cared for.

When a married couple discovers each other's primary love language and chooses to speak on a regular basis, emotions and love will be reborn. The love language, spoken in words of affirmation, often nullifies and washes away critical, harsh words. Language is always an act of communicating how the heart is feeling as well as what the mind is thinking. As the scripture says, as a man thinks, so is he.

We must learn to express love to each other by finding the love language that is so needed. The craving for love is our deepest emotional need whether we are women or men or children. After all, children are just small adults, if you please. If we feel loved by significant people in our lives, such as our partners or our mates, then the world looks so much brighter to us. But if it doesn't, we don't feel loved. Then a cloud of gloom hangs over our head. If we are running low on affirmation, if we question whether we are loved or not, as Gary Chapman phrased it, our love tank is empty. It all looks dark, very dark. More than dark, it looks alone and it feels alone, and thus our reflection will show in our behavior.

Empty love tanks make us feel rejected. Empty love tanks have to do with feeling connected, accepted, and nurtured. Connection requires the physical presence of people who say they love us and meaningful conversation and communication between those same people. Acceptance implies unconditional love regardless of how I behave, and nurturing is always feeding the spirit, the priest. And of course, comfort is the care you provide. The opposite of connection is abandonment, the opposite of acceptance is rejection, and the opposite of nurture is abuse—physically, spiritually, financially, or verbally. The wife that feels rejected, abandoned, or abused will almost certainly struggle with her self-worth. Then she begins to search for love in the wrong persons or the wrong places.

Negative self-worth and purposelessness are the result of feeling abandoned, rejected, and/or abused. Women need words of affirmation; again, we cannot emphasize this enough. These affirmations, of course, might concernmy behavior, physical appearance, or personality. They can be spoken, they can be written, but they must be expressed.

One of the languages of love is quality time. Quality time is so much of what is needed in a woman's life to heal her softly. Special time, time when there is just nobody but me and you, no kids, no phones, no friends, no relatives, no work. In fact, the Old Testament says when couples are married—God knew about woman when He created her—the man is to take a year off to fulfill all of her heart, fulfill all of her needs, and do everything she wanted him to do.

Give her all the time she wants in that year. Fill up her love reserve. I cannot say until she wants no more, because we never come to that point. But fill her up for that year; give her her desires so she'll be secure in your love, secure in your presence, secure in the future, and secure when you are not there.

Quality time is a language of love. Quality time is giving somebody your undivided attention. Quality time is your giving a part of your life. It is a deep communication of the language of love. The Bible even talks about acts of service. Exodus 21:10 says, "If he take him another wife; her food, her raiment and her duty of marriage shall he not diminish." In other words, if a man takes a wife he is responsible for her food, her clothing, and her "duty of marriage. None of these shall diminish or stop; they shall all continue. I looked up duty of marriage and the word duty. I found in looking up the original text, that there was no definition for duty under the Hebrew. I pondered and wondered in these three categories why there were no words to describe duty. And then I looked up duty in the Hebrew in OT:1686, OT:1696, and OT:1697 [what are these references?? You must be clear about what they are and where they are found – J. Dennis. I found out that duty in that sense was words and vowels you had spoken. Your duty is what you said you would do. What you spoke before God, spoke in the presence of witnesses, spoke to the wife you are about to marry: it was your marriage vows.

What you spoke becomes your duty, your obligation. I found out that duty also meant care, acts, work, service, an answer and communication. These are the duties that you are responsible for—not just the sexual act, even thought it is also a part of that.

Benevolence is caring for someone, so the Bible says in Exodus 21 to make sure she has her food, make sure you nourish what you have taken, make sure she has the strength to love you, to understand you. Make sure you feed her with proper nutrition so that she can build a strong back along with strong bones and cells to have a healthy relationship. For what you feed her is what she will become. We all know that what we eat is what we become. So God placed man in the position of feeding his family, to see that he nourish and cherish his wife so she can become a reflection of his glory.

He is to make sure that he has clothed her, and that she is properly covered with the raiment that reflects the glory of God, which is her robe of Jesus. Make sure you give to her the duty you promised; you promised to love her, you promised to nourish her, through sickness and in health.

Remember those vows, remember all those dreams, remember all those words that you said. Purpose to fulfill them by asking God to help you, and He will. After all, He wants His men to be a reflection of Himself.   The person who speaks the love languages is always looking for things to do for others, particularly forthe person whose primary love language is acts of service. Again, words might be empty if not accomplished by doing; "faith without works is dead." So there are many dead marriages, because there are no works to support them.

If he loved me, then he would help me. If she loved me, she would fix my food[Note: The above quote is from James 5:14 so it's not from Jesus, nor does it say to pray the prayer of faith and lay hands.]I love the way that Jews and Italians greet each other with a kiss, touching each other's face several times.

I often stand by and just watch this expression of love, not one kiss but several on each side, until the broadest smile breaks out on that person's face. Hugging and kissing are a way of filling the love tank and preparing one to receive life experiences of ups and downs.

Nothing is more important than a physical touch. A baby would die without constant physical contact. Anytime we stop touching, worse things are on the way. For instance, in the marital relationship, you know when couples no longer touch, when they sit far apart, when their feet don't meet in the bed anymore, when their hands don't touch as they walk, that things are not well. When the heart does not melt at the sound of his voice, we know that we are in need of a healing her softly experience.

A full love tank is ongoing. We fill each other's love tank with the primary love language of the person we are involved with by speaking their language to them constantly. Then like the high priest you can go into the holy of holies, and you can sprinkle each other with all these love languages, with appreciation along with affirmation. Yes! Telling each other how much they are needed, loved, and appreciated. And, of course, you can also let them know after affirmation, like the psalmist said to the Shulammite, "Come away with me, my beloved." And there you had the gifts of a beautiful wedding table where he performed acts of service, and his physical touch was so welcomed that it opened up her heart and her mouth as the shy and black Shulammite expressed in songs.

God values individuals. God said that everybody is somebody in His eyes. God forgives, and He forgives us when we act like we are nobody and most of all when nobody cares. He always cares.

He forgives me when I walk away from the greatest love ever given to me. When I leave to go search for love, leaving Him behind. And He will forgive me for rejecting Him. And when He does, we must promise to be someone in His life—His bride.

God loves you, woman of God. And He wants a relationship with you. God wants to affirm the love that He has with you, that He is always there for you. And He wants you to express His love for the power of the spoken word. We give gifts to God.

God is like us; He loves to receive gifts. He loves to receive tithing and offering, the times, the skills, the services. He loves to hear you say, "I love you." And we show our love to God by serving each other. No greater love has man than to lay down his life. Then God wants quiet time, quality time, and He wants to be touched by us. And He wants to touch others by us. God wants to affirm others and encourage others, and He wants to do the same for us. He wants us to experience life to its highest good. All God's words are found in worth and desire to build and to be in relationship with Him. The creator of heaven and earth, woman of God, is really in love with you. God speaks so fluently of His love toward man, His words of affirmation, from Genesis to Revelation.

The Bible pictures a loving God who declares His love by truth and comfort, salvation, redemption, healing and provisions—all for us. The love language, the words of affirmation, proceed throughout the Bible.

David, the second king of Israel, was so moved by God that he declared how sweet God's words were—sweeter than honey. He said he gained understanding through His precepts. David knew the highest desire, knew him as a provider, and a father, and he declared, Your statures are forever; this is not a one-night stand love, it is a forever love, and the joy of my heart and the joy of the experience of being in a forever love cannot be eradicated. I put my hope in Your Word. I know You are going to tell me the truth. I talk to You seven times a day to affirm our love in response to your communication to me.

David's primary vehicles for expressing his love to his God were hymns of praise, thanksgiving, adoration. Nobody could speak the way that David did. Thank God that we have the Psalms that we might use the same words to affirm our love to God.

God delights to affirm us. He said to us, Fear not, for you are mine, I will be with you when you pass through the waters. I will be with you when you pass through the rivers, I will be with you; they will not overcome you. Here is God's willingness to take care, willingness to talk and be there with us, in our times of need. He wants to abide with us, and He wants us to respond to Him for the love He shares with us. As Jesus promised His followers, they He would never leave them or forsake them, so God has promised that to us. He has rid us of the fear of abandonment.

Speaking of the language of quality time, Jesus focused His attention on the twelve, and He spent deep, quality time with these men, that they could experience His deepest personal love. Jesus was with them. He stayed with them. He showed them His love, He showed them His acts of service by leading them and by feeding them, as Martha showed her acts of service by cooking and Mary showed hers by sitting at His feet.

Quality time with God should not be a chore, rather it should be a time of rejoicing. It should be healing and powerful, un-interrupted as much as possible. Quality time is one of God's greatest gifts of the love language. Sometimes I just can't wait to be alone with my God. Sometimes my soul gets so thirsty just to be alone with my God. I must set apart that time, then I can be alone and refreshed in His presence. For in His presence there is fullness, and that is what quality time does for us as we come before the Lord, and for us as couples in each other's presence.

I am talking about more than simply being in a room; I'm talking about being in the presence of the heart, in the presence of the mind. I know that you are mine, and your thoughts are on me, about me, and toward me. You're thinking how to put a smile on my face how to win a deeper affection by your presence. There is fullness; my love tank will not be empty again. Our God is a giver God, a gift-giver God. He gave us every seed bearing plant on the face of the earth, every tree that had fruit bearing tree so that the seed could bring us increase. All beasts of the Earth, birds in the air, creatures that move on the ground, everything that has breath—God gave them every green plant as food. God saw all that He made, and it was good. He gave what was good to His man.

Remember, God still wants to give you what is good. Thank You, Jesus! Tell Him, tell Him right now, "God, You can give what is good to me and for me." Reciprocation and love and relationships are God-given expressions, just as He expressed His love to Solomon when He asked him, "What do you want, what should I give you?" Solomon responded, and then God, the great giver of gifts, said, "I will give you what you asked—a wise heart, a discerning heart, and there will not be anyone not like you among the kings. I will give you riches and honor in your life time and there will be no equal." God gave riches and honor. God gave wisdom and understanding. God gave the tools for life and life more abundantly, the spiritual life and natural life. As John 3:16 says, "For God so loved the world, he gave his only begotten Son, that whosoever believeth in him should not perish, but have everlasting life."

God gives gifts to those who love Him. Learn how to give and learn how to forgive. Learn how to lavishly give. How great is the love of God that the Father has lavished on us! All the languages of love have come together for you, affirmation, tenderness, quality time, intimacy, service, and healing.

His love is shown by giving gifts. And they're often material as well—houses, furniture, cars. He touches us and allows us to taste Him. He doesn't hold back food or clothing, a shoulder, our tongues, our prophecies, gifts of leadership and apostles and prophets, power gifts, such as healing and discerning. The giving of gifts is the primary love language. God is the giver of love.

Once when I was a little girl, I experience a Christmas with no gifts for me, and it scared me for the next twenty years. I remember getting up on Christmas morning. Everybody had one or more gifts under the tree—my sister, my brother, the two siblings that I lived with, but I had nothing under the tree. I remember crying so hard that I thought my eyes were going to cry blood. I cried until my nearly always drunken stepfather came out of his room. He wanted to know what was wrong, why was I still crying my heart out. The question was not really where was my present, but why was I not loved. For me, the present represented love. My sister had a coat, my brother had a watch, but there was nothing for me. My mother went in the closet and pulled out a white doll, wrapped a rag around her, and handed her to me with her hair uncombed. I felt exactly like that doll , and I refused to receive it, for in receiving that doll, somehow I thought I'd have a rag wrapped around me with unkempt hair.

I cried even the harder, because the gift that was being presented, in my eyes, did not represent me or love. And rather than having a secondary love, or an unconscious love, a hand-me-down love, I would not receive it at all.

My stepfather told my mother to put me in the car. He drove me to the only store open on Main Street, and he bought me a gorgeous black baby doll. She was beautiful, well dressed and manicured. That's all I had, that's all I wanted: an equal gift, a precious gift, a gift that represented love and me. And that is what you do when you give. A gift is a reflection of my love, but it is also a reflection of you. I remember walking round to my aunt's house to show off my doll. We lived in a small town, and it had been noised about Ann didn't get anything for Christmas; there was an ugly remark made: she didn't get anything because she was a bad girl.

It made me wonder how was I bad, but I quickly dismissed it; after all, I had the gift in my hand. It might have come late, but it was there and that was true. He wants to abide with us, and He wants us to respond to Him for the love He shares with us. As Jesus promised His followers, they He would never leave them or forsake them, so God has promised that to us. He has rid us of the fear of abandonment. Speaking of the language of quality time, Jesus focused His attention on the twelve, and He spent deep, quality time with these men, that they could experience His deepest personal love. Jesus was with them. He stayed with them. He showed them His love, He showed them His acts of service by leading them and by feeding them, as Martha showed her acts of service by cooking and Mary showed hers by sitting at His feet.

Quality time with God should not be a chore, rather it should be a time of rejoicing. It should be healing and powerful, uninterrupted as much as possible. Quality time is one of God's greatest gifts of the love language. Sometimes I just can't wait to be alone with my God. Sometimes my soul gets so thirsty just to be alone with my God. I must set apart that time, then I can be alone and refreshed in His presence. For in His presence there is fullness, and that is what quality time does for us as we come before the Lord, and for us as couples in each other's presence.

I am talking about more than simply being in a room; I'm talking about being in the presence of the heart, in the presence of the mind. I know that you are mine, and your thoughts are on me, about me, and toward me. You're thinking how to put a smile on my face how to win a deeper affection by your presence. There is fullness; my love tank will not be empty again.

Our God is a giver God, a gift-giver God. He gave us every seed bearing plant on the face of the earth, every tree that had fruit bearing tree so that the seed could bring us increase. All beasts of the Earth, birds in the air, creatures that move on the ground, everything that has breath—God gave them every green plant as food. God saw all that He made, and it was good. He gave what was good to His man.

Remember, God still wants to give you what is good. Thank You, Jesus! Tell Him, tell Him right now, "God, You can give what is good to me and for me." Reciprocation and love and relationships are God-given expressions, just as He expressed His love to Solomon when He asked him, "What do you want, what should I give you?" Solomon responded, and then God, the great giver of gifts, said, "I will give you what you asked—a wise heart, a discerning heart, and there will not be anyone not like you among the kings. I will give you riches and honor in your life time and there will be no equal."

Chapter 14

THE
ANN EVANS
STORY

HEALINGHER
SOFTLY

In the first chapter of this book I shared part of my story of getting to the place where I realized I needed to be healed. That chapter ended with my cry to God for help and healing. In this chapter I am going to go into more detail about what happened before and after that cry. James I. Evans was my first high school boyfriend, my friend, and my protector. He worked at our local grocery store, had his own car, and pursued me. The first time we met was at a school dance. I was not allowed to get in cars with boys—my aunt would kill me! So his brother drove behind us as James walked me home. I was impressed.

James would meet me at church; he bought me little gifts almost daily. For the first time since my grandfather's burial, when a cousin held me so closely and tightly, I felt safe! I thought I would be safe with him the rest of my life. I would not mind giving him my life and the two children we share—Keith and James I. Evans Jr.—forever. I married my husband when I was fifteen. As I said above, he was my first boyfriend, my knight in shining armor, and my protector. And I was having our love child. When I met him, I was a virgin. It was at the height of the Vietnam War, when everything was uncertain. Death was all around us. Every day someone was being drafted, and a month or week later we would hear that he had been killed in battle. That was what it was like to be alive during the 1960s. We were living in Camelot, and its walls were coming down. President Kennedy was dead; our beloved leader had been killed.

Love songs were at their height; all we had to look forward to was love and the beautiful songs of love. The Supremes were singing that some day we'd be together, and our moment was now. Our friends were all in love. We danced to "Up on the Roof" as we snacked on Coke, popcorn, and noodles with tomato sauce and pig's feet.

We had a ball; we did not understand poverty. We had love, friends, family, and a neighborhood that said we belonged. And we had to be somebody. That was what mattered to us.

It happened on prom night. James was older than I was. Several of us went out to Walkers Lake after prom. On the way back, the police stopped us and took James to jail for drinking and driving. Before that night he had never drunk, but that night Larry, a friend of James's, had poured beer over all the car and over us. It went everywhere. He did it as a joke. My brother was in the backseat, and one of the other teens drove the car home to my house.

Of course, we knew not to tell James's mother what had happened. His sister Essie was like us; she was fun and understood us. We knew she would help us, so about ten of us teenagers bounced over to her house at twelve midnight in tears.

James was her baby brother, so she came to his rescue. We all spent the night at the jail waiting for him to bond out, so at five a clock we all went to my house tired and scared, yet rejoicing that James was out, unfair as it was that he was arrested in the first place.

We were happy then. Everyone curled up in some corner of the house to rest until later that morning. The house on Spruce Street was a big, older, wooden house, so everyone found a place to rest. No adults were present—after all, they trusted us. After such a frightful night, the guys all had to go to work later that day, so a few hours' rest was OK. And what happened next was so beautiful and natural.

I wanted to comfort him, and he wanted to hold me. The next month I was sick—vomiting and all the other symptoms that go along with it. We never thought I was pregnant, because penetration was never complete. My mother sent me to the doctor, who assured her I was still a virgin. But the next month I was still sick, so she sent me back.

As a child, I had always had trouble with my stomach, so this was nothing new to my mother or me. But this time the doctor did another test—and this time the rabbit died. When he said to me, "Little girl, have you ever had something to do with a little boy?" I could have died on the spot with shame and embarrassment. To this day I do not know if I answered him. He told me my mother was on the way there, and he gave me a prescription.

I had to head my mother off, stop her from coming there. Much of the time we traveled with friends; in those days hardly anyone walked anywhere alone. My mother and I met by the Cuban store, with the fresh smell of Cuban bread, ham, and pickles. The smells were making me sick. This time I was not begging my mom for thirty-five cents to buy a pickle; no, I told her that the doctor said I just needed to get the prescription filled and I would be all right. When I asked her for the money, at first she said OK, but then an expression came over her face, and she said No; she was going to walk up to the doctor's office.

As I said above, in those days everyone walked everywhere. Within ten blocks one could be at the store, doctor's office, school—all on Main Street. And after she said No, fury exploded out of my mother.

She was only 5'4", and even though I was nearly 6', she was in my face. I walked very fast, yet she kept up with me. My friends left me as she called me names from Main Street to Spruce—whore, stupid, and other names. In between her yelling the whole neighborhood knew that Ann was with child; my mother was yelling and telling it to the whole world.

That was OK, though (or so I thought); I thought James would make it all better, but he left me, too. My world was crashing, and there was nothing I could do. What happened? How could I go to the school hop and see friends? Now I was all alone, feeling embarrassment and shame. My aunt said she did not want to see me; James's family said their plans were for him to go to school. My wicked stepfather told me I was a whore like my mother and that I would have a house full of illegitimate children. My mother was enraged; she was living her own failure over again through me.

I'll always believe that if I had taken those pills that the doctor had given me, my beautiful boy would not be here today. The Baptist church I attended wanted me to repent in front of the whole congregation; but I would not do so. After all, I knew all that happened there—lots of whoredom; my mother and stepfather had their friends, too. Here I sat alone with my thoughts—and with a new life growing inside of me. I was sick and alone, but I was excited. Now I would have something to love me good; this baby would not care that I was skinny with no hips. Remember, this was still the sixties, and curves and hips were in. I went through pity parties, abandonment, abuse, and everything you can imagine.

I went through it. But one day, on December 23, after nine months of being alone, Mr. James decided he wanted to get married! After nine months of being alone, now he was ready to marry me. But my mother told me that I did not have to get married now because I had already endured the shame.

I did not see much of him in that nine-month period; he had his own shame to deal with. Once we were all going to a football game. When we got there, he walked in front of me so that he wouldn't be "with me." That was my first time out with him after finding out I was pregnant. Friends did not stay around or come back in those days, because it was not hip or cool to be a teen mother. Yes, there were some, but they were considered bad girls.

I married James on January 7. I wish I could say it was a happy occasion, but I can't. My aunt signed for my permission to get married, and disappointment was all over her. James's sister signed for him, and the same sense of disappointment was there with her also.

And yes, I was disappointed too, but I had no choice. I had nowhere to go. I needed to leave my mother's house; my stepfather was worse than ever now that a baby was on the way. Living in the house was hell to me, and I was called every name in hell by my stepfather. When I marred James, something inside of me was very sad. Why did he wait so long if he loved me? Why did he let me go through this alone, with no moral support? Was he the same boyfriend who used to buy me little things all the time? Things like scarves for my long hair and pretty pins and stockings for church? We had shared ice cream and soda, and he was so kind to me. Now all that had changed.

I was scared. I did not know this person I was marrying, and words would not come out of my mouth. James did all the talking; I would just giggle at everything he said. When the time came to share my heart and fears, I had no words—or they just would not come out. I had always dreamed of my wedding day when I would wear a beautiful white dress; now here I stood in a courtroom with strangers at work and a gray dress on—not the happily ever after story every little girl always reads about and dreams of for her life.

Nevertheless, we were married, and I was going to work for the first time. I found a job with a government program that helped young people who needed jobs; the government paid half of the wages, and the employers paid the other half. They also trained their employees—including me. James got a job, too.

But now we had to find a place to live. We found a place in the housing projects and some old furniture. I thought we were set—a new apartment, lights and water, jobs for both of us, and a new baby. What could be better? For a while, things were pretty good, and then James got a car. And after the car came, we did not see him very much. He would come home later and later from work, and sometimes on the weekends he wouldn't come home at all. He would leave on Friday and we wouldn't see him again until Sunday. Something was happening, and I just knew it was like seeing my mother and stepfather all over again. But now it was happening to me and my baby.

James started coming home with the smell of alcohol on him. There were no more ice cream floats together. Instead I was alone with my baby, and even though I loved him, it was not enough. Not when my husband was coming home drunk. And then the beatings began.

For no reason James would come home late at night, and I would wake up and find he was beating me. And soon I heard about the other women. This was not my knight in shining armor. How could he treat me like this—beating me and having other women? Embarrassment set in, along with depression. I start to hate going to work, because everybody was talking about me or us. We all rode the city bus home from the hospital where I worked, so I heard all the gossip about us.

I soon lost my job for not showing up. James would beat me, and then I would stay up crying all night, depressed. I just could not go to work, and now I spent all the time day dreaming of a perfect happy life. James was happy—he had the car, the ladies, the time, and the money. I tried to drink, thinking that would keep him home with me. But it didn't; the drinking just made me sick and more depressed, leaving me throwing up and lying in my own vomit, too sick to get up for the bathroom. No, that was not for me, with the hangovers that made you wish you were dead.

James was leaving me. He no longer wanted to drink soda pops with me and go for a drive on the beach and neck in the moonlight. Now he wanted the party life, and he was not taking me; nor did I have the desire to go. James's new friends and lifestyle of course brought woman into his life. I was alone every weekend and crying my heart out, wondering what happened to the boy I loved and who I thought loved me. You know, the one who would stay up all night on the phone to talk to me, protecting me from my cruel, drunk stepfather. Now James had become the very person my stepfather was. It was like a nightmare; I was living the life of my mother after all.

My every thought over and over again was, What did I do? How can I get him to love me again? With his new lifestyle and new interests, the money stopped coming home. He would not pay the rent, and being in public housing, they started turning off one utility at a time. First it was the water. We had no water, and the baby and I had to borrow water from the neighbor. James was not there. He only came in at night, so not having water did not bother him. I hoped he would come in on Friday and pay the rent and the water would be turned back on. But he did not come home!

Frustrated, I took the baby and walked to my mother's house to bathe myself and the baby. That house held such pain for me and reminded me that I could never escape from the world of sadness and madness. It was getting late, and Mother was leaving. I had to go. She was leaving for the weekend, and her husband had begun his drunk.

My mother dropped me back off at my apartment. I saw with surprise that James' car was there. I went in to put the baby in his room and then to get the rest of the baby's things I had taken when we walked to my mother's house. I put them in the baby's room and then walked to our bedroom. When I got to the door, I heard music playing and saw a woman in my bed with my husband. I walked into the room and around the bed in disbelief—this could not be happening to me. *Why would he do this to me? I love him!*

But the words would not come out of my mouth. It was like I was somewhere else looking like this. I thought to myself, Men are like dogs. Dogs go after anything bleeding. My father abandoned me, my brother beat me, my stepfather hated me, my husband beat me, and now he was cheating on me in our house with the water off.

What's more, I heard ringing in my mind all the curses my stepfather had ever said to me— "You're nothing but a whore." Did I deserve this? Was I born to be in pain? James tried to rise up out of this woman's arms, but she pulled him back down. And he stayed there. I finally heard my voice say, "Excuse me," and I ran out of the bedroom to the kitchen, trying to breathe. For the first time in my life I wanted to hit back, so I looked for something to use. I picked up an iron. James came in, but I could not hit him. I threw the iron on the floor, and then he began to beat me. I was on the floor with him beating me with with his fist. I saw black. He was choking me, and I felt life going out of me. But it did not matter.

Suddenly I felt his hands lifting from around my neck, and I heard someone begging for my life. It was my mother on the floor with us. She had come in, why, I cannot say. After I had gotten the last things from her car, normally she would drive off, but for some reason she had come in. James picked me up from the floor and threw me out the back door.

I was carrying our second child, and lying in the dirt that night I thought, Is this all I am? My mother got the baby and helped me up. With my nose bleeding and broke and black eyes, tears could not come. She was taking me back to the house of pain, the house where my stepfather hated and cursed me and called me every name from hell. "Whore" and "bitch" were his favorite names for me. Who would wanted to be compared to a female dog, but now, with nowhere to go, I was on the way back.

Here I was, a high school dropout, one baby in arms, and my mother did not know one on the way. I was hurt and ashamed; I felt like dying. I thought my life was over.

What was wrong with me? People could not love me; worse, they wanted to hurt me or kill me. Every man in my life beat, hit, and left me; maybe it was me after all.

I knew the routine. My mother would leave for the week-end; she would say she had to work the weekend, but the truth was that she just couldn't take her husband's drunken stupor and cursing. I knew she had found a place or person of comfort. I would be left alone to fend for myself and my baby: old times with a new twist. My mother left, and my stepfather was nice to me at first, seeing my beat-up face swollen two times its size, nose out of place, two black eyes, and my neck looking like a price of rotten meat. I looked in the mirror and could not believe how bad I looked!

I still was wondering were James was and if he cared that he had hurt me. We would be the talk of our small world back then. I could hear them saying, "Did you hear what happened last night? She caught him in her bed with another woman, and he beat her for seeing too much?" How could I ever live this down? Would my face come back whole? I could not go to the hospital, because then they would arrest James. Who cared about my nose anyway? I was starting to feel like life did not matter anyway; maybe I would not wake up and that would be that. I was tried, and I went to sleep. But I woke up with the sound of my baby telling me he was hungry. I did live, and since there no one to take care of him but me, I guess I could not die today.

Nine months went by pretty fast. I did not see much of James. He came by to bring me my half of the furniture. Keith, my baby, cried for his daddy and ran after the car. For eighteen months he wanted his daddy. I walked him around to James's mother's house where James was staying.

He was dressing to go out. I felt no pain there; I thought, like the first pregnancy, I would not be seeing him.
My mother got me jobs cleaning people's homes. I walked there and walked home, and I lost about thirty pounds. My friends told me that I did not look like I was with child. My face healed, my hair grew, and my weight came down. I looked good, but I felt so unloved. Why couldn't he love me?

My mother's friends decided that it was time I was taught the game of life: what is sauce for the goose is sauce for the gander. They told me that it was time for me to go stepping out, so they fixed me up for the club and took me there. I had always wondered about places like that; now I was in one, eighteen years old. My mother told me never to order or drink anything but soda, to keep my head. My mother was a smart woman, and she was right about that.

The music was playing much like our school hops, and people were dancing. Smoke filled the air and covered the smell of my mother's toilet water perfume I was wearing. And then out of the blue a man came over and asked me if I wanted a drink! My mom's friends failed to tell me what to do in situations like this, so I looked at them for help. Asseis spoke up, "We are having sodas. Three, please." "If you want to talk to her, you got to go through us" was the message. He quickly left to do just that. He had just arrived back at our table when shots rang out. Asseis grabbed the keys, my mother grabbed me, and under the table we went—and the man with us. It was like they knew what to do. We stayed low and crawled to the door, me six months with child and the man begging my mother to let me stay, holding her and my hand. She gave me that shut up look, we were leaving now, and we made it to the car.

190

We went in and did not stop go until we reached home, with hearts pounding. So this is clubbing. I could see regret in my mother's face, and she never took me again.

I got down, and someone stepped on my chest, thank God not my belly. Somehow I was starting to think that this club thing was not for me. Maybe I should just stick to church. God has a way of keeping you when you do not want to be kept. So that's what I did. Even my mother's friend had to admit something was strange about of these events. So back to church I ran.

So many things were happening. I remember walking to a service and hearing a lady yell out from the second floor that King was dead. The baby inside of me moved when she said that. In my life so much death had occurred—first Kennedy, now King. What was this world coming to? Should I even be bringing life into the earthworld when there was so much pain and sorrow? James came by to see me, of course, in my ninth month, the day before the baby was born —just like he had done with our other child. He knew and the baby knew when their daddy was back in our lives, and they came. He came by that night after I had gone into labor that day.

My mother called, and he drove me to the hospital. I was in the labor and delivery room and looked out the window to see him leaving me in the hospital, and my pains stopped. I was not going to have that child without him. Of course, I was miserable now. The doctor wanted to know what happened after so many hours; then he induced labor. Two hours later his daddy was there. Maybe now he would love me.

Well, he had a good job with a dragging company, so he moved us out of the house of pain into our apartment. Oddly enough, it was the same complex where the lady had yelled that Martin Luther King Jr. was dead. I was happy to fix up that little place free of yelling. As you can see from this testimony, I went through the pity parties, abandonment, abuse, and everything you can imagine. I went through it. But one day I got saved—and not only saved, but also sanctified. And not only sanctified, but I also got filled with the Holy Ghost. And not only was I filled with the Holy Ghost, but I became beautiful. My ear was open to the living God, who told me, "You are fearfully and wonderfully made."

I didn't need any other Joe Blow to tell me that. I put my shoulders back, I lifted my head, I tucked in my butt—God Almighty could not lie to me. He would not lie to me. He told me I was the apple of His eye. He told me I was a good thing. He told me I was the workmanship of His own hand. That's what God said.

I had been told all my life that I was an ugly duckling. I was six feet tall—too tall to be considered "beautiful"—or so I had been told. All the negative things that had been said to me all my life now became unimportant. The King of the universe loved me; He was telling me I was the fairest of all—and I had no better sense than to believe that I was just who He said I was. He said that it wasn't my mother or my father who had begotten me; He had begotten me. He blew life into me. He was the one who said that I would be born on the twenty-third of September. It was He who said, "LIVE! You shall not die, but live and declare the wonderful works of God." And I believed Him.

My husband and I divorced in all this wonderful time, and then I got saved seven years later. Then Homeboy comes home. I was not looking for that; I was looking for a Boaz, but a has-been came. I rebuked and bound, but God said, "You can't rebuke Me, and you can't bind Me. This is what I have for you."Here comes Joe Blow, and he hasn't changed a bit. I prayed, "God, You have to do something! There's no change here." And He replied, "Oh yes, there is; the change is in you. You are more than a conqueror. The greater one is on the inside of you. And because the greater one lives in you, your breast is going to satisfy him all the days of his life."

So I began to prophesy to my breasts: "You will satisfy him. You will satisfy James all the days of his life. While he may get something 'good' elsewhere, it won't satisfy him, and he will come back to what satisfies!" So I closed and locked the door to the house. I took my children and myself. I was no longer depressed. I was no longer upset. God was washing out my wound; He'd brought me to the pool of Siloam.

Then James started coming around every Sunday morning to watch me go to church. I would not stay home from church. I would tell him, "I'll see you later, darling. I have to go see the King, but if you're here when I get back, I will fix you something to eat." I faced him with the confidence of the Holy Ghost. I memorized scriptures about what God said about me, and I believed them. I acted on those scriptures and waited on God to move. I didn't try to force James to change, and I didn't try to manipulate him. I just walked the walk and stood up straight; when it was time to play around sexually, I said, "I can't; I'm a holy woman. I would love to accommodate you, but I'm wife material." He said, "You've always been my wife."

I said, "I believe that, but do you? You have to prove that. You can't take me to my own bed, you can't take me to the Holiday Inn, and you can't take me to the judge. But you can take me to the preacher, because I'm Ms. Good thing. And the other side of Ms. Good thing is a wife." He started cussing me out and telling me he was going to leave me forever and find someone who would do what I wouldn't. I said, "That's OK, darling, that's your choice." He left, and I didn't see him for about six months. I was just happy in Jesus—speaking in tongues, going to church, and teaching my children about God. Then one day he showed up again. He said, "Well, I'm ready."

I answered, "Ready for what, darling?"
"I'm ready to get married, what do you think I'm ready for?"
"Is that a proposal?"
"You can call it whatever you want. I don't know why you're so happy about everything . . .
"It's the joy of the Lord. The joy of the Lord is my strength."
"I think you've just gone crazy with this church thing."
And I told him, "Honey, it's good for you; you just wait."

And now this same man and I have gone through everything—fighting, the whole nine yards, and much more besides. But today this man is my husband, my lover, my pastor, and my friend. It has not always been easy, but it has always been possible—and it's always been fun!

Chapter 15

HEALING HER SOFTLY

HEALINGHER SOFTLY

Now you've heard my story. You know that I have been "healed softly" by God's grace and mercy. And you can be, too. What hurts have you experienced? Have you been abused physically? Mentally? Emotionally? Have you been told that you are no good? That you will never amount to anything? Has your blood been spilled and poured out because of abuse? Let's take a look at Paul's letter to the Ephesians:

> Husbands, love your wives, even as Christ also loved the church, and gave himself for it; that he might sanctify and cleanse it with the washing of water by the word, that he might present it to himself a glorious church, not having spot, or wrinkle, or any such thing; but that it should be holy and without blemish.
>
> —Ephesians 5:25-27

In this passage, Christ tells husbands to wash their wives by the washing of the water and by the washing of the word. Often when I counsel with people who are in trouble, I make an appeal to the priest (the savior of the home). I ask them if they are willing to act out what Christ has commanded them to do wash their wives. The washing symbolizes the baptism, taking away the old to bring in the new, taking away the dust of judgment to bring the righteousness of Christ Jesus, removing the dryness and deadness of life and watering it with refreshing waters. The water heals, the water restores, the water cleanses, the water energizes, and the water oxygenates and refreshes. When the priest uses the water, which represents the authority of God, and his hands, which represent the healing of God, the bride responds with life hope, faith, and desire. And when that happens, it's time to experience the steps of healing.

196

Steps of Healing

The first thing to do is realize that people can make your world if you let them. Your world is framed by words, according to the Word of God. God framed the world by words (Gen. 1). The words that we speak and allow people to speak over our lives determine how our worlds are held together. That is why God let Adam call the first woman Eve, mother of the living; Eve, the representative of life, that which brings life and not death. So regardless of where her position was, what she was, her name was never altered by God or by Adam. She was continually to bring life to earth. Make sure that when you are named, you are named according to the Word of God. Sometimes we have to rename ourselves from the names that have been imposed on us, given to us by the people who have no knowledge of who we are or what we are, yet who have the authority to speak into our lives.

We must name ourselves according to the Word of God. It is such a dangerous thing in this time when so many women are being called with the B-word. The B-word means a female dog that happens to be bleeding, happens to be available to anything that passes her by. She doesn't breed anything but dogs, the lowness of life. So we must not allow ourselves to be changed from life into a mere dog. We must maintain our position of being Eve of living things—you cannot say believe without saying Eve. Therefore we must come to a new state, name ourselves, and cast off the names that have been given to us. We must name ourselves according to Spirit as well as the Word of God. The next thing I must do is frame my own world. God has given me this authority. In Genesis, God gave dominion to both male and female, then subduing power to both male and female.

He gave good gifts to both male and female, and He gave them authority—and we must use our authority. Even in the scriptures God allowed Adam to name the creatures the birds, the bees, the cattle, the giraffes, and to name Eve.

We see something so miraculous in the time of John the Baptist. Here we see a woman that was carrying a baby; then the angel came and told Elizabeth what the child was to be named. While tradition said that the child was to be named according to the name the father or somebody in the family, God had already named the child, given him his destiny. He gave John's mother the name of child so her world could be reframed. The child would bring about repentance, and his name had to be John, the beloved of the Lord.

You see, God will allow you to rename your world; you are the one who has to call it into place. You have to say, "I am a daughter of destiny; I am a woman who is blessed by God." You must know who you are. Your circumstances did not make you; God made you. Your circumstances did not create you; God created you. Your circumstances might have buried you in the mire and clay, but under that you are still uniquely you. Your circumstances made you part of the trash pile, but that is not your destiny. You are buried underneath all the trash, the diamond hidden just waiting to be discovered. All you have to do is arise out of the clay and mire by allowing the Holy Spirit to help you. Allow God to empower you; use your mouth to speak, saying who you are. Name yourself: "I am an Esther, I am an Ann full of grace and mercy, I am a daughter of the highest, I am a king's daughter."

Hebrews 11:3 says that through faith, we understand that the world was framed by the Word of God, so that things which are seen were not made of things which do appear. That's powerful. EFramed means in place or in time. It also means according to.

It means to charge things around you after the fact, mightily, particularly, absolutely. To frame means to compose, and it retains the application. So we can understand it means to charge time or place, to cause my time and my place to be charged by the words that I speak. We frame our worlds by the words we speak and by the words we allow people to speak into us. Isaiah 54:17 tells us that we don't have to receive anything.

Remember that the Word of God compares the words of a dog and a whore; they are of the same price. Actually, when someone calls you a dog, they are calling you a whore; they're synonymous. So, we have to cast off those words and reframe our world so they can fit and be charged by the words that we say. Remember what Isaiah tells us: No weapon formed against you shall prosper. Every tongue that rises against you in judgment, you condemn. Remember that two most vital women in the New Testament were Mary and Elizabeth. I will refer to these women often because they are the bearers and the carriers of the New Testament church. Elizabeth: old woman pregnant by the word of the Lord, whom God instructed as to his name: he was to be called John. A young woman who was carrying her Savior, her Deliverer. Her world would be changed by what she was carrying. These two women allowed their lives to be completely and forever changed, along with ours.

They chose to name what they were carrying from heaven instead of by the dictation of men. Mary could have allowed men to shame her. She was a teenager pregnant, unwedded, and in the eyes of the world, good for nothing. Mary's baby was introduced to the earthworld by angels who had already announced who and what He would be in heaven, in earth, and to mankind. The angels had already announced what John would beearth to men—Elijah, turning the hearts of many back to their fathers. I want you to also know that you have already been named, you have already been called. Heaven has a name for you.

The next step of healing is know what heaven has called you, what heaven has named you, and then line up with your name. Line up and be what heaven has called you to be. Heaven has not called you a female dog; heaven has called you a queen. Heaven has not called you defeated, but heaven has called you victorious. Heaven has not called you a second-class citizen, but heaven has called you a child of the king. Heaven has not called you ignorant, but heaven says you have the mind of Christ. Heaven has not called you to be broken, but heaven has called you to be made whole. Heaven has not called you to be locked up in a house of women, but heaven has called you the bride of the king. Heaven has not called you one of no worth, but heaven has said you were the royal diadem that will make up the king's crown.

Listen to what heaven has called you, and respond to that calling. Say the same thing that Samuel said: "Lord, here am I." Respond to your name. Respond to the Anna who lives in the house of the Lord, the temple, praying with Simeon that you might see the King of glory. Respond, and be a Deborah that you might lead the army into victorious triumphs. Respond as Esther, and be beautiful and have the favor of the king.

Respond to the women of the world and be used by your king. Respond to Eve and say, "After all I have been through, I can still produce a redeemer king." Respond like Ruth, that no matter where you been or who your family might have been, there is a Boaz waiting for you. Respond. Respond. Respond like Mary Magdalene; bring all your anointing and pour it upon the king.

There is a world waiting for you, and you can frame it by calling it by the name that heaven has called you. In this day and time we must be so sensitive to what God has said about us. We must be Mother Teresa in our day. We must understand that we receive gifts from God. And how do we receive gifts from God? By declaring like Mary, "Let it be done unto me, God, according to Your Word. Not my words, the devil's words, people's words, or society's words, but according to Your Word let it be done unto me."

God wants to enhance us and use us until we are channels of his love to others. God speaks the love language of gift giving, and He doesn't mind giving us whatever gifts we need to accomplish our tasks. When we give to others we reflect His love. Giving to others is a reflection of the healing love of our Lord and Savior. We are channelsthat carry the love of God to others.

Serving people equals loving God according to Matthew 25. Jesus is the life—Jesus is the life I want to live, Jesus is the life I want to express, Jesus is the joy I want to give, Jesus is my all and all. Serving people is what a loving God wants me to do and wants me to receive. Love always involves sacrifice and service. You are willing to love those who have no way to show it or give it back; to offer them your services is a message of love. The poor need the work of our hands.

The lonely need the work of our hands. The overwhelmed need the work of our hands. The sick need the work of our hands. The depressed need the work of our hands. And they also need the love of our hearts. The abundance of love and its expression—this is why Christ made a church. We must realize the connection between loving people and a loving God. This connection establishes the artery of heaven. God may beat His heart in heaven sending love channeled through the arteries that will disburse it here on earth.

We have to do the work, and the work is nothing unless we express our love for Him first. We do not do the work so that people might know us, but that they might know Him through us and by us. Acts of service and the words of Jesus—Jesus combined them both. When he was her on earth he said: "The Spirit of the Lord is upon Me because He has anointed me." He was anointed, and that same anointing is what we need today.

ISBN 10: 1-56229-054-1
ISBN 13: 978-1-56229-054-2

Pneuma Life Publishing
www.pneumalife.com
1-800-727-3218

Tune in and watch Ann Evan's Broadcast
program on 24 Hour Internet TV Network
www.annevans.tv